Another 40 days

of Faith, Family, Work, and Fun

Art Sathoff

1st WORLD
PUBLISHING

ANOTHER 40 DAYS
of Faith, Family, Work, and Fun

Art Sathoff

Copyright © Art Sathoff 2015

Published by 1st World Publishing
P.O. Box 2211, Fairfield, Iowa 52556
tel: 641-209-5000 • fax: 866-440-5234
web: www.1stworldpublishing.com

First Edition

LCCN: 2015932995
ISBN: 978-1-4218-3721-5

Acknowledgements

I want to thank First World Publishing for making the experience of having my books published agreeable and hassle free. The founder of First World, Rodney Charles, has an interesting story of his own—from monk to *New York Times* best-selling author to small town publisher. I am thankful to have met Rodney!

Thank you, also, to my former administrative colleague Marci Dunlap, who graciously agreed to write the foreword to this book. Marci has a love of writing and a teacher's heart years after she left the classroom. When I decided to write my first book, I think Marci was as excited as I was. For that I am very grateful.

Finally, thank you to our older son Jordan, with whom I have had many great conversations about values, work, and leadership, and to whom I owe a debt of gratitude for good feedback and editing.

Foreword

Man Thinking

A few things are true and always will be. Life is complex. There will be storms. A person can choose to live in panic, disorientation and oblivion, or they can choose to approach those complexities with grit, humor, and reflection, as author Art Sathoff does. Sathoff's *Another 40 Days* offers readers a chance to find the most profound lessons for personal growth throughout the web of daily life. As I read *Another 40 Days*, I heard the author's voice and anticipated his actions. Sathoff's writing creates the desire to wring as much knowledge out of life as possible. In the world of education, it's easy to lose oneself in theory and the daily grind, and even easier to lose oneself entirely. This book reminds everyone that if we are to give 100% to whatever we do, then it is critical to reflect and prioritize what is always important. Sathoff, our modern-day Emerson, seizes **Man Thinking**, the epitome of a rich and effective learner. What is to be gained out of reading *Another 40 Days*? A desire to reflect. An urge to do more and be better. A need to work with professionals as self-aware as Art Sathoff. For those who do not think there is time to read...slow down. Do it. There are pieces of the past that will benefit your future.

Marci Dunlap
Fairfield CSD Curriculum Director

Day 1:

Lessons Learned

Clearly one of the most beautiful things about being human is our capacity to grow and learn. It is widely stated that parents are children's best teachers and that the home is where the most important education takes place. This is the way things are supposed to happen. Sadly, many people stop growing for a variety of reasons, and many parents abdicate their responsibility to teach their children. I learned a lot in my home, and those lessons have helped to make me the person I am. Let me share some things I learned from my immediate family:

From My Dad: **Enjoy Life!**

My father, Craig Sathoff, was always quick with a smile or a joke. I grew up hearing his laughter. Sometimes his jokes were so corny, but he got a kick out of them, which made the rest of the family smile, too. For example, multiple times

I heard him ask a waitress for "liquefied Brazilian beans." I'm pretty certain no one else ordered coffee that way in an average waitress's day. Another "punny Craigism" originated with his commonly known nickname "C.E." Almost without fail, when he wrapped up a conversation with a former student or acquaintance in Iowa Falls, he gave a hearty, "I'll be C.E.in' ya'!" That had way more flair than saying, "I'll be seeing you."

Dad's love of life was not restricted to bad jokes. He was never more at home than at a card table with friends. I'm pretty sure I was the only little kid in my circle of friends playing Bridge and 500 at home. We had some rousing games of multi-player solitaire and Hand and Foot with family and friends, too. If you were my dad's partner in 500 or Bridge, you could just assume that you were not going to get the bid very often (He would because a standard bid in 500, no joker required, was "eight no trump.") and your team would either dominate or go out in a blaze of glory. My dad apparently believed it's a lot more fun to play offense than defense.

I have so many good memories of backyard ball games with my dad and siblings, great home-cooked meals around the large oak table, road trips in search of antique treasures, lawn darts and croquet, family vacations, and many other light-hearted moments. I learned how to enjoy life from my dad, who spread good cheer wherever he went.

From My Mom: **Serve and Be Humble!**

Many of my childhood memories of my mother are of her doing things for others. I remember her reading to me, tucking me into bed at night, making me breakfast, and generally keeping the household running on an even keel.

Her locus of control seemed to be centered on the home. It was from the home that she ran the family's antique shop, shipping items all over the country long before anyone had heard of eBay, thanks to *The Antique Trader*. Mom worked very hard at home and also did her share of waitressing in her early-married years. She was a "stand by your man" kind of wife for my dad, and she was proud of her kids, too. She never seemed to think about herself much; she was always focused on serving others.

Mother Mary was humble to a fault, too. It almost broke my heart to hear her say, late in her life, that she had not really made much of her life. Mom had married at just seventeen years of age, and she and Dad were young parents. Mom and Dad had their family of four children complete by the time Mom was 27. It is true that my mom only attended college for a year and that she never had what some might consider a career. She was a wonderful Christian influence on her children and others in her life, though. She was an inspiration to many as she coped with the death of her husband, her own paralysis, and recurring bouts of cancer. She was the strongest person I ever knew, but in her humility she didn't recognize her greatness.

My mom wasn't too good to speak to anybody, and she helped anyone she could. She passed away in 2007 and lived in Iowa Falls, Iowa, her whole adult life, so you can understand why I smile when mail with her name on it finds its way to me in Indianola in 2014. "What kind of mail?" you ask. The Sierra Club, Smile Train, Muscular Dystrophy Association, Feed the Children, Save the Wolves, and any other group you can think of that could ask for a buck must have gotten one from my mom. She had a servant's heart, and she knew it wasn't about her. These are lessons I have tried to internalize and bring into my personal and professional life: serve and be humble.

From My Older Brother Ed: **Work Hard!**

I cannot adequately state the incredible impact my older brother Ed has had on my life. I am five-and-a-half years younger than Ed is, and I watched him closely as we were growing up. He played on Iowa Falls's first boys' basketball team to go to the Iowa State Tournament, and that became a mission for me to follow in his footsteps. Ed was an excellent basketball player, and the biggest reason for that was his incredible effort. He was not a superior athlete. In fact, he had been a sickly child with severe allergies, and even in high school they kept oxygen on the bench for him! "Sweaty Eddie," as some called him, was a workhorse, though. I would compare him to Kurt Rambis on those great Lakers teams of the 1980s, and I don't think Ed would object to that. He was a garbage-collecting, pump-faking, elbow-throwing machine; and truthfully, my game wasn't all that different although I was a little bigger and a little better leaper. I loved trying to emulate my older brother and trying to catch up with his feats.

Ed was a driven student, too, and I came close to achieving the academic success he had in high school and college because I could see how hard he worked and how important it was. I still remember my advanced biology teacher in high school telling me, "I haven't seen anyone hack the hell out of a cat like that since your older brother." It's true: dissection was not a strong point for me and evidently not for Ed although he did become a doctor. There were those who doubted he could do it, and I'm sure that drove him more.

To this day Ed works extremely hard. He is a partner in a mental health firm, and he has worked and built the practice from the time he left medical school. I typically talk to him on a weekend, and more often than not he tells me he needs to head in and catch up on dictation. My brother Ed is one of those guys that you like to see do well because you know how hard he has worked, yet he has remained genuine and down to earth. I hope you have had the good fortune to have someone set a positive example of the value of hard work for you. I could not have asked for a better example than Ed.

From My Older Sister Laura: The Value of Friendship

My older sister Laura has always enjoyed getting together with friends, and I have noticed that she has had some very enduring friendships. Laura has had some pretty serious health issues, and there have been quite a few times when she needed assistance to get to an appointment or to make it to one of her kids' events. Her friends always came through. That shows me that she has cultivated good friendships, and people want to help her.

Laura always was social, and she enjoys getting together for celebrations. I think she inherited her love of the get-together from our dad, and she has his culinary ability, too. She understands that happy moments are to be shared, and her close friends have shared many of those moments through the years.

I don't necessarily form close friendships easily, but I definitely have people I could call on for anything and people I have shared a lot of good times and laughs with. My closest friends are people I have worked with and raised our children as they raised theirs. I always say my big rocks are faith, family, and work. I don't include friends on that list though my friends come from those three sources. Everyone needs friends to lean on and to share with, and that is something I have learned from my sister.

From My Younger Brother Robin: **Be Yourself**

Robin has had some very interesting experiences, and I used to consider him the black sheep, or non-conformist, of the family. He has traveled the world and been places I have never been and most readers never will go. He has been to Africa, has lived on a kibbutz in Israel, backpacked through India around the time of their big earthquake, was in Nepal when the royal family was assassinated, and I'm sure I am just scratching the surface here. To my knowledge Robin had nothing to do with the earthquake, the assassinations, famine in Africa, or unrest in the Middle East though he's certainly seen it all!

Robin is an artist at heart, and his sketches done when he was backpacking through India and Nepal have been published as a book, *Xenophilia*. Even while he has done other work, such as being a psych screener in a prison, Robin hasn't lost his creativity and love of art. His art is a great way for him to be himself.

Wherever he has been and whatever he has done, people always like and appreciate Robin. I think one very big reason for this is that he is genuine, and he simply is who he is. People are attracted to other people who are like that. It took me a little while to learn to be myself, something that seems to come very naturally to Robin, but once I did, life became a lot more enjoyable. This seems like a very simple thing, but there are a lot of people in the world wearing masks or trying to live up to others' expectations.

My hope for these people would be that they could learn to relax and be themselves like my brother Robin.

From My Adopted Brother William: You Can Re-create Yourself

Billy Joe Barker came to our family as a foster child and was adopted as William Joseph Sathoff. My parents welcomed a lot of foster children into our home through the years, and Bill came not long before I went to college and then went to work. I didn't get to know him as well as I might have, and I'm sure I wasn't as nice to him as I should have been.

Being a foster child has to be a little unsettling, coming into an established home and trying to figure out where one fits in. In many cases there are definite reasons foster care is necessary, but leaving one's birth family and home has to require a huge adjustment. In Bill's case, he was old enough that patterns of behavior and personality characteristics were well engrained. He really had to re-create himself when he came to live with us.

Obviously the adoption brought a new legal name and identity for William, too, and he has kept that name. Now he is married and has a child, so he is contributing to the continuation of the Sathoff line. Bill still takes opportunities to re-connect with his adopted siblings. Today he continues to re-create himself and write his story as a family man and provider.

I have experienced this re-creation process myself. My values and behavior are not what they once were. I credit God and my wife Cindy for that. My heart aches for people who have given up and think it is too late to have a new, better life for themselves. Even though I have been skeptical of "jailhouse conversions" like most people have been, I love the story of the thief on the cross, who recognizes Jesus' divinity and who receives the promise from Jesus: "Today you will be with me in Paradise" (Luke 23:43).

I encourage you to take a few minutes today to reflect on lessons learned. Make a list of family members or people you grew up with, and write down what you learned from them. You might even surprise yourself with the results! God bless you.

1. _____ taught me_____

_____

2. _____ taught me_____

_____

3. _____ taught me_____

_____

4. _____ taught me_____

_____

5. _____ taught me_____

_____

Day 2:

To Every Thing
There is a Season

This morning I had the privilege of officiating at the memorial service of a long-time teacher and church member. This duty was what I was least prepared to do as a minister, and it undoubtedly is one of the most important duties clergy have. It is important to help people say good-bye and move on, and being able to truly make the service a celebration of life is something that only comes through faith. I always ask God to speak to me and through me and to give me the words the family and friends of the departed need to hear. I always seem to end up emphasizing that no one understands all of the mysteries of life and death, but we have a God Who makes and keeps promises, and of that we can be sure.

I think there is a unique power in the short graveside service that often follows the funeral service in church. First of all, those who have attended the visitation or service out of obligation typically do not make it to the graveside. I don't mean that in a snotty way; I've been on that side of the equation more than once. What I mean is that there is an intimacy, gathered around the gravesite, usually with just the closest family and friends.

Today was a beautiful day in late May in Iowa. The temperature was in the upper 70s, there was a breeze, the sun peeked in and out of the clouds, and the birds were singing. Ecclesiastes 3 was one of the Scriptures I dipped into for the graveside service (See Appendix A). It was the perfect backdrop to consider the seasons of our lives and the plans God has for each of us. I believe God gives us nature not only as a way to enjoy and appreciate His creation but also as a model and way for us to understand our lives.

In farming country, as planting season concludes, people can understand what John 12:24 means: "Very truly I tell you, unless a kernel of wheat falls to the ground and dies, it remains only a single seed. But if it dies, it produces many seeds" (John 12:24, NIV). This is the way God intends it to be, and this is why believers can accept death not as the end but as a new beginning. When a believer dies, it is a soul harvest for God. It is extremely comforting to know that the loved one who has passed is not gone but is a part of the "great cloud of witnesses" that surrounds us (Hebrews 12:1, NIV).

I used to love to teach a poetry unit, and one thing we did was read different poems about death since that is a universal theme that many excellent poets have delved into. Metaphysical poet John Donne's "Death Be Not Proud" was always a favorite of mine (See Appendix B). The students and I usually decided that the theme was something like, "Death, you're not so bad!" I love the reminder to death,

"Thou art slave to Fate, Chance, kings, and desperate men," and also the reminder that, "one short sleep past, we wake eternally."

It is my personal belief that once we take the sting out of death (another image courtesy of Donne), then we can focus more on life: how we live it and how we can enjoy it. Medieval Christians viewed this life as only a preparation for the next life. Now, I'm not sure they were the cheeriest bunch, and I believe that God intends us to enjoy our time on earth, but I wish everybody believed and understood that we are just visitors here and that what we believe has eternal consequences. The alternative is to just put in our time here on earth or to hope for the best, being pawns of circumstance. That kind of fatalism is what Shakespeare's Macbeth was feeling when he said in Act V, Scene 5,

> "Life's but a walking shadow, a poor player
> That struts and frets his hour upon the stage
> And then is heard no more: it is a tale
> Told by an idiot, full of sound and fury,
> Signifying nothing."

Probably the best thing that outlook provided was a great title for William Faulkner's classic novel *The Sound and the Fury*. I recommend the book; I do not recommend living your life with this outlook. It is impossible not to feel like an actor in a cosmic (maybe even badly written) play sometimes. There is much that is beyond our control and much we do not understand. This is where the believer has an advantage. We know how the story ends, and it is a very happy ending! I have heard it said that it is important to know your Bible, but it is even more important to know the Author.

I trust that God knows what He is doing and that He gave me this life for a reason. That faith is bolstered by the fact that if it were not so, I could have died a dozen different stupid ways through the years! That's not to say that God did not favor anyone who suffered an untimely death. Part of the mystery of life is not knowing when the end will come. It's cliché, but we should be living like our life will end tomorrow because we can't be sure that it won't.

I don't want to be a downer on Day 2 of the book, and I hope thinking about life and death does not depress you. If it does, consider taking a close look at your life and where you think it is leading you. Like the great ancient Greek philosopher Socrates said, "The unexamined life is not worth living." Live your life like God intends it, and it will be very easy for people to make your funeral service a celebration of life! Remember, "The Lord will watch over your coming and going, both now and forevermore" (Psalm 121:8, NIV).

How would you sum up your views on life and death?

Day 3:

Nicknames

I am a nut for nicknames. I probably had no choice. I grew up in a family in which my dad called my older brother Ed "Rough and Ready Eddie," my older sister Laura "Laura Lynn, the Little Girl with the Great Big Grin," my younger brother Robin "Rockin' Robin," and me "Artie the Party Boy." These weren't just cute little family pet names; I think everybody in town knew our nicknames. I'm pretty sure they trickled out through every ninth grade English and creative writing class my dad taught.

I can't say I thought a lot of my middle school nickname "Stickman," but it certainly was appropriate. I looked like a goofy, emaciated early adolescent who was sporting a wavy mini-fro and wearing dark plastic glasses that had been broken playing basketball and taped back together with athletic tape. Wow. That's all I have to say: wow. God bless whoever nicknamed me "A-Train" after NBA player

Artis Gilmore when I was a budding freshman basketball talent! I just ran across a bunch of classmates' senior pictures recently, and it was a lot better reading notes addressed to "Train" or "A-Train" than it would have been to read, "Hey, Stickman..."

I have subjected my co-workers to a lot of nicknames. Some are obvious, but it's fun to have a name that has a story or joke behind it. Inside jokes amuse me, and my theory on humor (which my family, friends, and co-workers know) is that as long as something amuses me, it's still funny. I could call the high school office at my last school and ask to speak to Dale Dobeck, and the secretary didn't miss a beat in connecting me to the principal. Of course, he calls me Brennan. If you are lost at this point, I suggest you watch *Stepbrothers* at your earliest convenience. Other former administrative colleagues are known as Cheffychanga, Tri-egg, FTG, Rain Man, Petty Cash, Tiny, and Chip, just to share a few examples. There's a story behind every name.

I really am kind of childish sometimes. If I don't have a good nickname for you, I'm probably going to make fun of the college you attended or joke about your being a redneck. I think this probably would surprise some people, though, because this treatment is really reserved for those I am closest to. We all have our different identities, and nicknames just add to it. It's kind of like being in a club.

I'm happy to have the nicknames I have. My wife and older son both kid me with job-related nicknames, calling me "The Big Cheese" and "P.O.C." ("Pillar of the Community"). They call me those things to rib me a little, but there is respect in there, too. A diminutive colleague whom I kidded about being short called me "Superstein" and "Preacherstein," nods to my size and occupations. I appreciate the humor, and it's not everybody who has seen a Halloween JibJab video with Frankenstein lumbering around with his own face.

Nicknames are really just a small part of one of my non-negotiables: I am going to enjoy my work. It also goes right back to that lesson I learned from my dad: enjoy life. It is so important to have a sense of humor, especially a self-deprecating sense of humor. I know my students appreciated that about me when I was a teacher. Being able to laugh at ourselves helps keep us humble and keeps us from taking ourselves too seriously. Peter Ustinov says it well: *"It is not ourselves, but our responsibilities, that we should take seriously."* I used to have that as my email signature. Oscar Wilde probably goes a little too far when he says, *"Life is far too important a thing ever to talk seriously about,"* but I do like his spirit of fun. If you want a non-stop farcical, dry humor laughfest, read Wilde's *The Importance of Being Earnest*.

I strongly encourage you to inject a little humor into your life if you aren't doing so already. One easy way to do that is with nicknames. Take a little walk down memory lane. What are the best nicknames you have ever been called or have ever heard?

Day 4:

The Simple Things

Are you a person who values the simple things in life? I am probably more materialistic than I should be, and I like nice things, but I also really value some of the simple things in life. For example, I really like being able to take an hour and go walking on the trails with my wife Cindy. I should note that this is about the extent of my exercise, so this time takes on added importance. I would rather walk and talk with her than go to a fancy gym or have a personal trainer, though.

It seems like the things that really make an impression on us and stick with us are the simple things. I know my dad loved small town life, working in the garden, going to church with his family, sitting down to a good home-cooked meal, watching the fireworks and balloon races, and any number of other small-town, simple life activities. A website I ran across quoted him: "Craig E. Sathoff said that 'Hometown is more than just a town, it is a way of life, a place of peace and quiet, and when I return it is as if I have never been gone, and in my heart I have not.'" That's why he loved Iowa Falls, "The Scenic City," and lived in that small Iowa River town his whole adult life. That's why he took his family back to visit tiny Titonka, Iowa, frequently and was chosen to be the grand marshal in the town's centennial parade. My dad was the quintessential small town guy. If you want to see him expressing this in poetry, see a few of his poems in Appendix C. They are readily available on the Internet though he died in 1999.

My family and I are simple, small town people, too. Cindy grew up in Allison, Iowa, and Jordan and Trey have resided in Sigourney, Packwood, Richland, "Suburban Linby," and the outskirts of Fairfield. We love having a caring church family, knowing the people we run into on the street, and seeing the seasons change and the crops in the field.

Ask my sons about favorite childhood memories or homes, and they will mention things like picking up refundable cans and rocking out to "Jack and Diane" in the old Dodge Shadow or walking through the pasture to go to the timber behind our old 1900 stucco home we had in Richland. We have had some good vacations and nice things, too, but there truly are things money can't buy.

I firmly believe that one of the most precious gifts we can give to people is our time. I know I don't regret a moment I get to spend with my wife or sons (even if it's cleaning out gutters, a crappy job I detest but one that both boys help me with). As many people have stated one way or another, "No one ever said on their death bed, 'I wish I had spent more time at the office'." I am thankful I get to spend quite a bit of time with my family although I have quite a few meetings and the boys are on the run a lot. When I get the opportunity, I am always glad to relax at home or go out to dinner with family. There is nothing Cindy and I enjoy more than sharing a laugh with the boys, and they make us laugh a lot!

I have been involved in time-consuming pursuits, but thankfully, they have often been family affairs. For example, my wife and I coached basketball together for eleven years. We got really good at coaching or running a scoreboard while holding or feeding a baby. It's amazing how good of a playpen a big ball rack is for a couple of little boys, too. I wouldn't trade a minute of those crazy, busy days with my young family although I might not have the energy for it today!

I encourage you to think about things you do or could do that don't cost a dime but bring a lot of enjoyment. Here's a short list. Add a few of your own; then make time for them!

1. Take a walk, especially with a friend or loved one.

2. Check out a book from the library and read.

3. Watch a ball game with a child or spouse.

4. Play a game of Cribbage or a board game.

5. Go to church with your family.

6. Call or visit an old family friend.

7._____

8._____

9._____

10._____

Day 5:

Highs and Lows

Not too long ago I read a book by Seth Godin called *The Dip*. It reinforced some things I know instinctively and some lessons I have learned. These are not novel ideas, but they are worth remembering: challenges bring opportunity, adversity reveals character, and it's okay to struggle sometimes. I will delve into each of those statements in a moment, but let me return to *The Dip* briefly. Many people have heard of and experienced an "implementation dip," where performance temporarily declines as a new skill or change is being implemented (I am currently in a 35 year implementation dip with my golf swing). The implementation dip would be just one example of what Godin explores with *The Dip*; I encourage you to read the book. One of the best lessons I took from it is that <u>the Dip is your friend</u>. It creates scarcity, which creates value. In other words, not everyone is willing to persevere and grow through the Dip, so those who do so become a hot commodity!

Another very simple little book on this topic, written as an allegory, is *Peaks and Valleys* by Spencer Johnson, M.D. (author of *Who Moved My Cheese?* as well). I recommend this quick read, which encourages a mindset that helps us fully appreciate the peaks in our lives while learning to make the valleys not so long and not so deep. For me, personally, this process is assisted amazingly by my knowledge that the God of the mountains is the God of the valleys. See Appendix D for Lynda Randle's great song lyrics on this theme.

People who lose faith in the valleys or who fail to give God credit on the mountaintop are subject to chaos and wild mood swings as they traverse peaks and valleys. For some people life is much more of a roller coaster than it needs to be or should be. There is a good cautionary tale in 1 Kings Chapter 20 of the Bible. Israel's army up in the hills had trounced the King of Aram. As is sometimes the case, advisers tell him what he wants to hear. "Don't worry," they say, "their gods are gods of the hills. Wait 'til we get them on flat land!" (my paraphrase of 1 Kings 20:23-24). You can imagine how that turns out. "The man of God came up and told the king of Israel, 'This is what the LORD says: 'Because the Arameans think the LORD is a god of the hills and not a god of the valleys, I will deliver this vast army into your hands, and you will know that I am the LORD'." (1 Kings 20:28, NIV). I won't make that same mistake because "I believe in a hill called Mt. Calvary." See Appendix E for wonderful lyrics to that song by the Heritage Singers.

I intended to write about my three main points before now—challenges bring opportunity, adversity reveals character, and it's okay to struggle sometimes—and maybe I have been. The ideal behind these three statements is captured well by the Apostle Paul in his letter to the Romans: "Not only so, but we also glory in our sufferings, because we know that suffering produces perseverance; perseverance, character; and character, hope. And hope does not put us to shame, because God's love has been poured out into our hearts through the Holy Spirit, who has been given to us" (Romans 5:3-5, NIV).

I can't say it better. Being determined to persevere is an even better mindset than trying to end on a high note although I can't help but smile when I think of the *Seinfeld* episode when George Costanza announces, "Well, I'm out of here!" and exits on top whenever something goes his way or he makes a witty comment. I suppose there is some value to having a sense of timing. "Quit while you're ahead," is good advice casino goers should follow, for example, if they ever get ahead.

I'll finish today where I started, with a mention of Godin's book *The Dip*. While he stresses the value of persevering through the dip, he also writes that it is important to realize when you're headed toward a cliff or a cul-de-sac. In those cases, know when to quit and move on. *Discernment* is what I would call that, and that is a biblical principle that eludes a lot of people. Maybe I'll write about that another day. Until then, don't get rattled by peaks and valleys. Understand that God is with you in all circumstances, and He is molding and equipping you for greater things!

Day 6:

Words

I was with a guy in a professional setting today, and he got so excited when I used the word *antithesis*. He was happy to be with a person who appreciated and used words like he did. I wasn't trying to impress him or convince him that I was erudite, and I don't claim that *antithesis* is some kind of obscure, arcane word that makes me a smarty-pants. In fact, I get annoyed with pseudo-intellectuals who are just trying to impress others and sometimes misuse or overuse the word they are trying to impress with. In this case *antithesis* was just a fitting word for the point I was making. I mention this exchange because I get a kick out of how much the gentleman appreciates words and the power of language, just as I do.

Words do matter, and this is no new idea. Edward Bulwer-Lytton wrote, "The pen is mightier than the sword," in his play about Cardinal Richelieu in 1839, and I don't believe that is any less true today. The words of our nation's leaders project an image to the world. You can decide yourself if our country is more or less respected than it used to be and whether or not that impacts our nation's status and security. Authoritarian governments seek to control the Internet and social media outlets like Twitter because they know language can fuel a popular movement. Public figures in the U.S. have learned that saying the wrong thing can get them suspended, fined, fired, or ostracized. Language is powerful.

I gained an appreciation for words at a young age, listening and watching as my English teaching poet father used them so effectively. He could always elicit a smile or tug at the heartstrings with his poems. I also learned the joy of reading from my mother, who read to me and was always reading a book herself. Of course, reading is the best way to build a vocabulary.

I remember sitting at the Red Rooster, the little café across the street from our house, working the Jumble in the *Des Moines Register* with my dad. It was pretty exciting to be able to unscramble a word more quickly than my learned father—just another way my competitive fire was stoked, I guess. Games of Hangman weren't infrequent either, and I know I killed a little time as an English teacher with Hangman or Scategories, too, though I'd probably have to deny that to my staff in our Common Core aligned, assessment crazy public school environment today. I always wrote a different quote on the board each week and had weekly vocabulary study, and some students actually enjoyed it!

When I became a principal and didn't have the same classroom contact with students, I instituted a "C" Lunch Scrabble game in my office with a few students. What kind of self-respecting teenager voluntarily goes to the principal's office over lunch to play Scrabble? Great kids, that's who! I went to the wedding of one of them a couple of days ago.

A robust vocabulary and an exquisite turn of phrase comprise an effective arsenal for a person. Who wants to be the person who thinks, "Oh, that's what I should have said!" fifteen minutes after leaving the room? Wouldn't it be a lot more fun to have a nimble mind and a rapier wit? Our facility with language governs our ability to express ourselves and to think quickly in so many situations. Words matter, and Mark Twain, no stranger to a clever turn of phrase made that point well: "The difference between the almost right word and the right word is really a large matter—'tis the difference between the lightning-bug and the lightning."

I always feel badly for people who are at a loss for words and frustrated by communication. My paternal grandma, a very bright lady who taught English for years, was that way after she had a stroke. She got so frustrated when she either couldn't dial up a familiar word she sought or when she physically could not vocalize a word she knew. I marvel at the fact that Helen Keller, born deaf and blind, became able to express herself beautifully and powerfully. I also really admire people who are bi-lingual or multi-lingual. It really is inexcusable that my foreign language knowledge is basically limited to German Christmas carols and Spanish curse words!

I have been writing about the power of words, primarily in a positive vein. I have to confess that I have spoken carelessly on many occasions. I have hurt people. I have said things I regret. The Bible is clear about the power of the tongue:

"The words of the reckless pierce like swords,but the tongue of the wise brings healing" (Proverbs 12:18, NIV).

"The tongue has the power of life and death, and those who love it will eat its fruit" (Proverbs 18:21, NIV).

"When we put bits into the mouths of horses to make them obey us, we can turn the whole animal. Or take ships as an example. Although they are so large and are driven by strong winds, they are steered by a very small rudder wherever the pilot wants to go. Likewise, the tongue is a small part of the body, but it makes great boasts. Consider what a great forest is set on fire by a small spark. The tongue also is a fire, a world of evil among the parts of the body. It corrupts the whole body, sets the whole course of one's life on fire, and is itself set on fire by hell. All kinds of animals, birds, reptiles and sea creatures are being tamed and have been tamed by mankind,but no human being can tame the tongue. It is a restless evil, full of deadly poison. With the tongue we praise our Lord and Father, and with it we curse human beings, who have been made in God's likeness. Out of the same mouth come praise and cursing. My brothers and sisters, this should not be" (James 3:3-10, NIV).

The wisdom of Proverbs and the imagery of James just about nail it, don't they? The tongue can be a blessing or a curse. I think we know which one, the positive or the negative, makes a bigger impact, too, don't we? I have heard that it takes anywhere from 7-10 positive interactions to reverse one negative interaction.

Rotary's *Four-Way Test of the things we think, say, or do* provides an excellent reminder to use language (even our internal monologue, or our thoughts,) responsibly: "Is it the truth? Is it fair to all concerned? Will it build good will and better friendships? Will it be beneficial to all concerned?" That's a pretty high standard!

My mom's advice was a bit simpler but equally valuable: "If you can't say something nice, don't say anything at all." I think she also shared the folksy reminder, "You catch more flies with honey than with vinegar." Today Ephesians really convicts me when I read, "Do not let any unwholesome talk come out of your mouth," (Ephesians 4:29, NIV) and "Nor should there be obscenity, foolish talk, or coarse joking," (Ephesians 5:4, NIV).

I have made my living with words, as a teacher, coach, school administrator, and pastor. I have kissed the Blarney Stone, which is said to confer eloquence (more colloquially, the "gift of gab" or ability to B.S.), twice. I have had many people express thanks or appreciation for something I have written or spoken. I have greatly enjoyed writing a couple of books. There is power in words!

There is a special, divine power in THE WORD. The Bible is The Word in print, written by divinely inspired human authors. Jesus is The Word made flesh, God incarnate—a perfect God who took on human form to interact with His creation. This creation exists because God spoke it into existence. Don't let anyone ever tell you words aren't important!

I encourage you to read, to write, and to try to find joy in words. Improving your vocabulary does not have to be drudgery. Read authors who do great things with words, like William Shakespeare or Mark Twain. Write down quotes that you run across that seem to have special meaning for you. Improving your lexicon might do more than just increase your appreciation of literature or your ability to write and speak well. There might come a time when you have just the words someone needs to hear when he/she is hurting, confused, or discouraged.

Consider starting a list of favorite words, new words, or words people should know. Work a new word into your vocabulary every now and then. You might feel like a neophyte at first, but you won't be a troglodyte in the long run!

I list a few website suggestions below. Feel free to send me a game request for Ruzzle or Words With Friends or come visit me for a rousing Scrabble game!

Linguistically yours,

A Bibliophile

http://www.world-english.org/improve_vocabulary.htm

http://www.merriam-webster.com/word-of-the-day/

http://www.brainyquote.com/

http://www.biblegateway.com/

Day 7:

Uncommon Sense

Common Sense isn't dead (See Appendix F). It's not even on life support. It's just heavily sedated, staring up through murky water, trying to focus on the light that shimmers far above. In an era when we are constantly redefining the "new normal," maybe what's called for is Uncommon Sense. Maybe if we take a little different view of the traditional things we know to be true, Common Sense can retort like the great Mark Twain (Samuel Clemens) once did, "Reports of my death have been greatly exaggerated!" We really do not need to go through contortions to achieve this new perspective. There are three well-known concepts that can guide us to an uncommon level of common sense in today's world: empathy, reframing, and the balcony view.

Empathy is cited as an important 21st century skill by a number of business and education thinkers. Thomas Friedman's book *The World is Flat* made the case for empathy compellingly in 2005. Empathy is essential in the global community we live in today. In an age of multi-national corporations, electronic communication, social media, and outsourcing, there are no boundaries. Fewer and fewer people live in isolation in our increasingly diverse world. How can we function as citizens of the world without empathy?

Empathy is, as Harper Lee's folksy lawyer character Atticus Finch said, "Getting in someone else's skin and walking around for a while." I have experienced many situations where people just wanted to feel heard and understood. For example, as a school administrator, I have encountered parents who did not agree with an administrative decision and employees who could not be granted what they wished. Of course, they wanted the solution they desired, but in most cases it was very helpful for them to know I had heard their concerns and understood, even if I could not give them what they wanted. As a coach, sometimes I fielded playing time concerns. Parents or players did not always judge ability as I did. If they knew I understood the desire to play and the frustration of not playing, it usually helped build some trust in my judgment. As a parent, a friend, and a pastor, there have been many times when someone has been hurting and there wasn't much I could do. Merely being present during their pain and extending some understanding can be a great comfort.

The key to empathy, as Atticus (of *To Kill a Mockingbird* fame) knows, is to be able to put oneself in someone else's place. To do so requires an ability to see things through different lenses, often called "reframing" in leadership literature. Lee Bolman and Terrence Deal explain the concept well in their book *Reframing Organizations*. These authors identify different frames, or views, that leaders of organizations need to be able to transition between: structural, human resources, political, and symbolic. The frame that the leader is viewing a situation in guides the leader's decision-making and actions. A leader's facility in choosing the appropriate frame and his/her ability to utilize different frames greatly impact his/her effectiveness.

Sometimes a frame allows a person to get a little needed distance from a situation. One term for this distance is *a balcony view*. I am sure we have all had interactions with people who simply could not be objective or were too emotionally involved in a situation to be rational. In these situations it might seem like these people lack all common sense when in reality their speech and actions make total sense when looking through a lens of narrow self-interest. What they—and all of us—need is uncommon sense: the ability to step back, take a breath, and suspend our human tendency toward self-interest.

If we believe that we are created in God's image, that we have a little spark of the divine in us, then the task becomes seeing other people and difficult situations through God's eyes. Of course, we are not omniscient or omnipotent; we are time-bound, and we aren't capable of perfect, unconditional love. But are we willing to try? Are we willing to exercise uncommon sense in an age when common sense seems so hard to come by? I think we can, but it's something we have to work at.

What are some difficult situations or people in your life right now? Practice the art of empathy in a safe place right here:

Person or Situation_____

How they see the issue_____

_____

Person or Situation_____

How they see the issue_____

_____

Person or Situation_____

How they see the issue_____

_____

Day 8:

Authority

This morning I have been reading and thinking about Luke 3 and 4, which discuss John the Baptist preparing the way for Jesus and then Jesus' baptism, temptation, and early ministry. The more I study the Bible, the more the truth of Providence, God's divine plan, is reinforced. God had a plan for Jesus, and Jesus was perfectly attuned to it (even on the eve of His arrest, when He prayed in the garden to see if there was any alternative to His crucifixion).

I am intrigued by the reactions people had to Jesus. On a human level I understand how the Jewish religious leaders felt threatened by Jesus because His message undermined their power and the status quo. I can see how His followers expected Jesus to be an earthly king who would deliver them from Roman oppression. I appreciate the wonder (and at times bewilderment) His disciples had as they walked with Jesus in His ministry. The gratitude and love of those who were healed and converted makes sense. The reaction I find most interesting, perhaps, is expressed in Luke 4:32: "They were amazed at his teaching, because the message had authority" (NIV). This is reminiscent of His first visit to the Temple, when He impressed the religious scholars at age 12. So what was it; what was that special something that compelled even Jesus' critics to recognize His authority?

As I am writing, I am thinking of synonyms for Jesus' authority. *Credibility* comes to mind. People believed in Jesus. They trusted Him. He was credible to even those who hated Him. That's why He was such a threat. His family was the slowest to come around; they thought He was crazy at first. His hometown also struggled to see Him as more than the carpenter's son. Sometimes people have to hit the road to fulfill their calling. Jesus certainly did.

Another word I thought of was *ethos*. When I taught public speaking, *ethos* was a term that referred to a speaker's credibility with the audience. People are more likely to listen to someone they trust. This trust comes from recognition of the speaker's knowledge, experience, concern, or values. *Ethos* is a Greek word meaning *character*, and that meaning is well preserved in our language as we speak of *ethics* today.

During the Presidential election cycle we can be sure that the talking heads on television will be bandying about the word *gravitas*. This word has a Roman etymology and refers to doing something with dignity or seriousness. If the candidate is a male, he might be called a *statesman*. There is some kind of unquantifiable standard of being *presidential*. I consider this to be a largely superficial measure of appearance. Jesus was not concerned with this. He had true <u>authority</u>.

Where did this authority come from? Confidence is attractive to people, and Jesus had total confidence. He proclaimed in the synagogue, "Today this scripture is fulfilled in your hearing," (Luke 3:21, NIV) after reading Isaiah's prophecy about the messiah's actions. He told the crowd, "I'm the guy." He personifies the idea that truth cannot be denied when it is seen. Of course, He should be recognized this way because He said Himself, "I am the way and the truth and the life" (John 14:6, NIV).

There was a process in coming to this authority. We read, "And the child grew and became strong; he was filled with wisdom, and the grace of God was on him," (Luke 2:40, NIV) and "And Jesus grew in wisdom and stature, and in favor with God and man" (Luke 2:52, NIV). We see Him being baptized, receiving God's stamp of approval on His ministry, which Luke tells us began when He was almost 30 (Luke 3:21-22). Before His public ministry begins, Jesus has a wilderness experience where He is sorely tempted and tested (Luke 4). He emerges strengthened and gets about His Father's business. He knew exactly what He was doing and why. He knew exactly who He was. He had the confidence of experience and results, faith in action. In a word, He had <u>authority</u>.

It is the Christian's mission to become more Christlike. Any Christian, actually any person, can learn from how Jesus lived His life. He had a sense of purpose. He studied, taught, learned, and grew. He communicated with His Father, and He ensured that He had quiet time. He felt compassion and met others' needs. He cared about others and served others. He boldly proclaimed the truth. He overcame temptation. He suffered. He changed the world.

The more attuned we become to God's will for our lives, the more authority we will have. I'm fond of a quote I gleaned from Rick Warren a while back: "God will get you where He wants you to be with the influence He wants you to have." Believe that and enjoy the trip.

Reflect a little right now.

Ways I feel God might be calling me or nudging me to action:

1._____

2._____

3._____

Day 9:

Father's Day

This weekend people will celebrate Father's Day, possibly with gifts of ugly ties and backyard barbecues. My thoughts are taking me beyond celebrations to what it means to be a father. I reflect on my own dad, and I'm sure I see his imperfections as my sons see mine. I see the love of life he had, too, though, and I hope I inherited that from him (along with my squeamishness, claustrophobia, and total ineptitude with anything mechanical).

I see some of myself, good and bad, in my sons today as well. I know they love God and love their mother like I do. I know they understand the importance of working hard and treating people right. They exhibit and appreciate a good sense of humor like their dad does, and they probably don't cross the line into obnoxiousness quite as often as he does. They appreciate a good game or healthy competition and are typically good sports (Insert previous underlined comment here as well.).

My heart aches for people who have not had a loving father in their lives. Too many dads are absent, distant, or totally distracted. Obviously these "fathers" have no idea what they are missing and no sense of the legacy they are passing on. **Because there is a legacy.** Just as children can learn to love others, serve God, work hard, value friendship, be honest, be polite, etc. from a caring parent, they can learn to be selfish, uncaring, immoral, dishonest, addicted, isolated, dependent, etc. from an absent or self-absorbed parent.

I remember almost losing my dad in the fall of 1988, the year I began teaching. I was so sad that I wouldn't be able to talk about being an English teacher with him. I was crushed that he wouldn't get to meet Cindy or know his future grandchildren. As I look back, I know I was focused pretty selfishly on my future and myself that I thought he wouldn't get to be a part of. Cindy met my dad in ICU that Thanksgiving. She was by my side during his six-month stay at University Hospitals; we went to a Christmas Eve service with him there, too. I am one of those blessed individuals who had an incredible father and has a wonderful wife, who gave me a couple of pretty remarkable sons!

My dad recovered from his illness and lived another decade before dying in an auto accident. He got to see Cindy and me marry and have Jordan and Trey. He and Mom got to see Cindy and me coach together, got to see me inducted into the Iowa High School Basketball Hall of Fame, and undoubtedly got to see the lessons they had taught me as a child lived out until Dad's death in 1999 and Mom's in 2007. I feel my parents' presence and influence in my life more strongly today than ever before. This is why I wrote that my heart aches for people who have not had a loving father.

Parents who don't love and instruct their kids miss out on some of the biggest joys in life, and they don't fulfill duties that are Biblical and part of God's plan. Children who do not have loving parents have an uphill battle as they try to figure out life on their own and search for significant adults who can be surrogate parents. I know my parents understood this, as they were foster parents for many years.

At the risk of sounding like a writer for Hallmark cards, take the time to let your family know you love them! I love mine, and I hope I get to be that funny old grandpa some day. My parents were awesome grandparents, and Cindy's parents certainly are, too!

Check out Appendix G for another Craig Sathoff poem about fathers, and take the time today to re-connect with your family.

Day 10:

Disappointment

What is it that makes disappointment so disabling for some people while others seem to routinely get up, dust themselves off, and jump back into the fray? Maybe people who aren't resilient haven't watched enough John Wayne and Clint Eastwood movies, where the protagonist routinely takes a beating but perseveres and prevails in the end. There could be other reasons. Maybe people who fall prey to disappointment lack a particular skill set, learned behavior, or outlook, which could enable them to deal with—and profit from—disappointment. I am going to attempt not to be too repetitive of Day 5 (Highs and Lows) and to that end, I will try to stick to my hypothesis that there are skills, learned behaviors, and outlooks that can enable people to effectively handle disappointment rather than be paralyzed and defeated by it.

Skill Set:

Having analytical skills dramatically lessens the emotional impact of disappointment. Rather than focusing on the pain of unrealized goals or the embarrassment of plans gone awry, analytical ability allows one to examine the reasons why the failure occurred. Identifying the underlying reasons for a disappointing result enables a person to be strategic in future efforts so that a more satisfying outcome happens. That sounds easy. Of course, there will be forces beyond one's control that can contribute to failure. There is also the possibility that new problems will crop up once the old ones are addressed. At the very least, being analytical will help keep people out of the trap of doing things the same way over and over and expecting different results (Einstein's famous definition of insanity). The old proverb, "Fool me once, shame on you; fool me twice, shame on me," comes to mind. People are going to make mistakes and encounter disappointments in their lives, but they don't have to make the same mistakes over and over and over.

Learned Behavior:

I think the most significant learned behavior to combat disappointment is perseverance. Keeping our eyes on the prize helps us endure the momentary discomfort and the inevitable setbacks. Everyone knows the story of the tortoise and the hare and the moral of the story, "Slow and steady wins the race." That's not a flashy bit of advice, but it is often true. The Bible is full of practical advice and encouragement to cultivate this learned behavior of perseverance:

"And let us run with perseverance the race marked out for us. . ." (Hebrews 12:1, NIV)

"We want each of you to show this same diligence to the very end, in order to make your hope sure" (Hebrews 6:11, NIV).

"By standing firm you will gain life" (Luke 21:19, NIV).

"Blessed is the man who perseveres under trial, because when he has stood the test, he will receive the crown of life that God has promised to those who love him" (James 1:12, NIV).

"And as for you, brothers, never tire of doing what is right" (2 Thessalonians 3:13, NIV).

And one final, practical note from Ecclesiastes—"I have seen something else under the sun: The race is not to the swift or the battle to the strong, nor does food come to the wise or wealth to the brilliant or favor to the learned; but time and chance happen to them all" (Ecclesiastes 9:11, NIV).

I haven't researched the religious beliefs or faith life of famous people to any large degree, but perseverance is often a key to their success. Michael Jordan being cut from the varsity team in high school has become an often repeated illustration of perseverance and drive for improvement. Even during his illustrious professional career Jordan's approach was to take any perceived weakness and work on it until it became a strength. People who followed his career could point to a vastly improved jump shot and a commitment to becoming a defensive stopper. The myth of natural talent ignores that the people at the top of their profession have universally persevered, sacrificed, and worked to become successful. Abe Lincoln's path to the White House is also famously held up as an example of perseverance. The following rendition is taken from nedhardy.com

Abraham Lincoln never quits.

Born into poverty, Lincoln was faced with defeat throughout his life. He lost eight elections, twice failed in business and suffered a nervous breakdown.

He could have quit many times – but he didn't and because he didn't quit, he became one of the greatest presidents in United States history.

Here is a sketch of Lincoln's road to the White House:

1. 1816 His family was forced out of their home. He had to work to support them.

2. 1818 His mother died.

3. 1831 Failed in business.

4. 1832 Ran for state legislature – lost.

5. 1832 Also lost his job – wanted to go to law school but couldn't get in.

6. 1833 Borrowed some money from a friend to begin a business and by the end of the year he was bankrupt. He spent the next 17 years of his life paying off this debt.

7. 1834 Ran for state legislature again – won.

8. 1835 Was engaged to be married, sweetheart died and his heart was broken.

9. 1836 Had a total nervous breakdown and was in bed for six months.

10. 1838 Sought to become speaker of the state legislature – defeated.

11. 1840 Sought to become elector – defeated.

12. 1843 Ran for Congress – lost.

13. 1846 Ran for Congress again – this time he won – went to Washington and did a good job.

14. 1848 Ran for re-election to Congress – lost.

15. 1849 Sought the job of land officer in his home state – rejected.

16. 1854 Ran for Senate of the United States – lost.

17. 1856 Sought the Vice-presidential nomination at his party's national convention – get less than 100 votes.

18. 1858 Ran for U.S. Senate again – again he lost.

19. 1860 Elected President of the United States. (nedhardy.com)

Thomas Edison, perhaps America's best-known inventor, was a person who absolutely understood the value of hard work and perseverance. I hope you can benefit from some of his thoughts:

"I have not failed. I've just found 10,000 ways that won't work."

"Many of life's failures are people who did not realize how close they were to success when they gave up."

"We often miss opportunity because it's dressed in overalls and looks like work"

"Genius is one percent inspiration, ninety-nine percent perspiration."

"If we all did the things we are really capable of doing, we would literally astound ourselves."

"The three great essentials to achieve anything worth-while are, first, hard work; second, stick-to-itiveness; third, common sense." (goodreads.com)

What do you think Michael Jordan or Abraham Lincoln or Thomas Edison would tell you about disappointment? I'm pretty sure they would tell you to quit feeling sorry for yourself and get back to work. That is a learned behavior, though, and you have to learn how to take your lumps then get back into the fight.

Outlook:

Obviously one's outlook, attitude, or worldview is going to greatly influence one's skill set and behavior, too. If one believes that losses are rarely fatal and that there is opportunity in the midst of difficulty, then one is more likely to persevere and learn from momentary obstacles. Being able to be somewhat stoic, not exactly detached but being able to distance oneself from the emotions of a situation, can help a person avoid decisions that result from clouded judgment. The ancient Stoics, a group of philosophers, carried this to an extreme. They held apathy as their highest ideal, so I think you can see that I am recommending just a dose of stoicism. Another philosopher whom I certainly wouldn't advocate following too closely from what I know of him is Friedrich Nietzsche, but I think there is a strong message in his often quoted expression, "That which does not kill us makes us stronger." If we have that outlook, we can begin to see disappointments and difficulties as something that will benefit us by testing and strengthening us. Anyone who has met a goal or accomplished something through hard work and determination has experienced deep satisfaction, even if there were times during the process that he/she thought the effort was going to kill him/her.

There are a lot of other quotes and people we could put forward that capture a desirable outlook. Legendary football coach Vince Lombardi is reported to have said, "It does not matter how many times you get knocked down, but how many you get back up." Chicago Bears legend Coach Mike Ditka said, "You're never a loser until you quit trying." I think this mindset of learning to enjoy a challenge and recognizing that life is full of them is central to learning to deal with disappointment in a positive way. I encourage you to do a check of your skill set, behavior, and outlook in dealing with disappointment. Maybe you will be encouraged by how well you are doing, or maybe you will find you need to do an attitude check or build some skills. You can use the simple chart below if you like:

Disappointment	My Reaction	Result
1.		
2.		
3.		

Day 11:
Prayer Changes Things

"Prayer changes things": this simple statement adorns the wall of the bathroom in our house. I hadn't really thought about its placement before today. Is it there to remind me to whisper a little prayer before I step on the scale? Is it a plea for regularity? I remember learning in college that Martin Luther suffered from frequent, severe bouts of constipation, and he had some of his greatest revelations in the W.C. (water closet). That's bathroom for us 21st century readers. But I digress. . .boy, do I digress!

Do you believe prayer changes things? I believe in the power of prayer, and I certainly have had times in my life when I feel prayers have been answered. I also have had the Garth Brooks "Sometimes I thank God for unanswered prayers," moments. Prayer does change things. It does not always change circumstances or deliver what the person praying desires. In 2 Samuel 12 we see King David, a man after God's own heart, earnestly praying for his son to be spared. When his son dies, David cleans himself up and goes to worship. Prayer doesn't always deliver what we want. It's not about changing God's mind or getting Him to deliver a miracle (although He can and sometimes does). Prayer changes and equips the people praying.

Understanding how to pray, committing to frequent prayer, and feeling the power of prayer are all things that develop over time with practice in a person's spiritual walk. That is not to say there isn't beauty and power in a child's simple prayer, but prayer is a spiritual discipline just like Bible study and worship are. We see Jesus modeling prayer, seeking a quiet place to commune with His Father on multiple occasions in the Bible. Jesus instructed His disciples how to pray, and a billion people or more say the Lord's Prayer, or Disciples' Prayer, today (See Matthew 6:9-13). Jesus tells His disciples He will do whatever they ask in His name (John 14:13), and this is at the heart of understanding prayer, I believe.

What can we really rightly ask in Jesus' name? Is it okay to pray for a lottery win? Most people would probably think not. Can we ask God to deliver us from suffering or difficulty? Surely God doesn't wish us to suffer, but I would think twice about this prayer, too. I think it was Rick Warren that said once, "God may send you a storm at age 30 so you can handle a hurricane when you are 60." No one likes to go through hardship although the Apostle Paul pointed out that we should be thankful for trials because they strengthen our faith(Romans 5:3-4).

When in doubt, look to Jesus. As He faced the cross and prayed in great anguish in the Garden of Gethsemane, spiritual anguish that had Him sweating blood

(Luke 22:44), He prayed to God to provide another way if possible, but He concluded, "Not my will but thine, Lord." We should frame our prayers that way: "If it is Your will, God." God's will and plan are perfect, and we see only in part (1 Corinthians 13:12). Ideally, we should be praying for strength, praying to feel God's presence, and praying for good to come out of our struggles. We should trust God's promises: "And we know that for those who love God all things work together for good," (Romans 8:28) and "For I know the plans I have for you, plans to prosper you and not to harm you," (Jeremiah 29:11). It's just tough to hold on to these promises when we're going through the fire! That's when we need them the most, though.

If you find your prayer life lacking or you find yourself doubting the benefit or importance of prayer, I encourage you to dive into what the Bible says about prayer. Some verse(s) will reach out and grab you! Go to http://www.openbible.info/topics/prayer and you will find 65 Bible verses about prayer compiled. That's a quick way to start.

The last couple of years, as I have led a congregation in a weekly time of prayer, I have found myself coming back to two ideas: there is power in a righteous person's prayer (James 5:16), and we should worry about nothing and pray about everything (Philippians 4:6). I don't pretend to have everything all figured out, and my prayer life isn't what it should be, but I know in my heart that **prayer changes things**. I pray that you will experience that certainty in your life. If you don't know where to begin, personalize the prayer below:

Dear God,

Thank you for the blessings in my life. Today I am especially thankful for _____,

_____, and _____.
Give me strength as I face trials. Right now I need Your help with _____.
Watch over those whom I love and be with those who are suffering. This day I ask for a special blessing on _____. Thank you for loving me, and I pray I will have a daily walk with You. Amen

Day 12:

Redemption

Have you ever been to a redemption center for cans and bottles? I have been in a few, and they typically are sour smelling, ill-kept spaces. Of course, as is true with anything else, there is danger in generalizing. The last redemption center I was in was actually pretty pleasant. That particular type of business seems to come and go quite a bit, reliant on volume since the business owner receives one cent per can or bottle. Cash flow can be a problem, too, since the owner is paying out money while collecting a big enough cache of cans to ship off. I think can redemption is a good thing, though.

When I was an enterprising young scrounger, I collected many a can from ditches and car washes for pocket change or moped fuel. My older son Jordan even remembers us slowing the old Dodge Shadow to pick up discarded cans to turn in later. I even picked up cans while my wife Cindy and I walked the country roads sometimes. I'm sure there were more accomplished can men or bag ladies than I was, but I did my part for the environment and local redemption center owners.

Isn't redemption wonderful? It takes the old, cast-off, forgotten item and gives it new life. Something that is seemingly trash ends up having value. The concept isn't limited to redeemable cans and bottles. Our son Trey has done quite a bit of "scrapping" the last five years, redeeming junk metal at scrap yards. Maybe it is due to growing up around my parents' antique shop and going to rummage sales with my mom, or maybe it's because I grew up always looking for the forgotten coin on the street, but I love the idea of finding value in what others have overlooked.

You know that's a Biblical concept, don't you? The Bible says there is joy in heaven when a lost soul is saved (Luke 15:7). It tells us the widow tears her house apart looking for the lost coin and rejoices when she finds it (Luke 15:8-10). The shepherd leaves the 99 sheep he has to look for the one lost sheep (Luke 15:4-7). The physician comes to heal the sick, not the healthy (Luke 5:31). This is VERY good news for us since we inevitably have times that we feel lost, forgotten, worthless, or unloved. God loves us. He is close to the broken-hearted (Psalm 34:18). When we turn to Him, He responds like the loving father of the prodigal son (Luke 15:22-24), with great rejoicing! Yes, redemption is wonderful.

I had the honor of performing two baptisms today, the last day of serving as pastor at Fairfield First Christian Church. What a blessing to participate in the most important redemption! Now these were nice people I baptized, and I would certainly not compare them to dusty old cans lying in a ditch! The truth for all of us, though, is that we will never be what we could be and will never come close to knowing God's Will for our lives until we make the choice for Christ and are baptized into the fellowship of believers.

It is important to note that Christian baptism gives the believer brothers and sisters in Christ. Baptized Christians are part of an important team (one that even Jesus the Son of God is a part of). Someone who has been baptized into the body of Christ should never feel like he/she has to face life alone again.

As I write this entry, on Father's Day 2014, the San Antonio Spurs have a 3-1 lead over the Miami Heat in the NBA Finals with game five tonight. They are on the verge of enjoying their own athletic redemption after nearly defeating the Heat in last year's finals. I have been greatly enjoying the Finals (even though I am a Bulls fan), and it is obvious that the San Antonio Spurs understand a few things about teamwork. They play excellent team defense, and they share the basketball so well that scoring looks easy. They scored 70 points in one half against the Heat and made 18 of their first 20 shots that game! I have not researched the faith lives of those Spurs, but I know they are enjoying redemption on the hardwood, and they understand the power of teamwork.

I believe that God expects us to learn from things we encounter in our everyday lives. If that weren't true, I don't think Jesus would have spoken the way He did to the people He encountered. I don't think He would have spoken in parables about crops and vineyards, sheep and shepherds, kings and beggars, and all of the other ordinary, real-life things that He did.

I know I have learned the value of a second chance in relationships I have and work I do. I have experienced the joy and power of a second life, being born again in Jesus Christ. I view myself as a reclamation project of sorts myself, and I am intent on making sure that I have been redeemed for a purpose.

I invite you to give a little thought to redemption today. Is there a relationship you are part of that needs a little TLC? Do you have some underutilized junk around your house that could enjoy a new, more useful life somewhere else for someone else? What is your prayer life like? Are you engaging in regular worship? Is Bible study a key part of your life? You can be both an instrument of redemption and the recipient of redeeming grace, and that is God's plan for His followers.

People/things I can help redeem: _____

_____

_____

Places I need some help myself:_____

_____

_____

P.S. The Spurs did win the title tonight, and Tony Parker commented after the game, "We just wanted to redeem ourselves." And ESPN posted, "For the San Antonio Spurs, redemption never felt so sweet," on Facebook.

Day 13:

Humor

I hope you have people in your life who make you laugh. One of my non-negotiables is, "I am going to enjoy my work." I have awesome co-workers who help to ensure that happens. Last Friday my secretary turned up in a gray wig, wearing a robe and pushing a walker, to escort me to a going-away potluck at our office. This get up <u>could</u> have been in response to the occasional comment about "women her age" and the periodic reminder that she is older (however slightly) than I am. I told her, truthfully, that she made a very good-looking old lady. For the record, I am gray-haired myself, and my cousin remarked that a picture my wife posted of us on Facebook, one that was taken for a church directory, looked like a "daddy-daughter dance" photo. That little sucker is only eighteen months younger than I am, but he has aged very well.

This morning I was the unwitting target of a complex sting. My auxiliary services director (Fred) has a habit of leaving his briefcase sitting, lid open, on the front counter of the office. There might have been a few times that the briefcase turned up in the women's bathroom or closet shelf when left unattended. Fred, locally revered as FTG (Frederick the Great), has taken this in stride, with amazing patience really. Boy, did I underestimate his deviousness.

When I walked to the front counter for a standing meeting this morning at 8:15, there sat Fred's briefcase, lid up, blocking my aforementioned wonderful secretary from the view of the public. Other employees were at the counter for the meeting, but Fred was nowhere to be seen. I have convinced myself that today I merely planned to move the briefcase to the side though this cannot be verified. I picked it up, and all heck broke loose: screaming bells and flashing lights that only I wasn't expecting! I quickly replaced the briefcase to its spot on the counter, on top of a sensor pad, as I examined what previously had appeared to be an ordinary package sitting next to the briefcase.

FTG stepped around the corner and said, "Art, you just made my day." I didn't swear or do anything too embarrassing, which was good, because Fred's next comment was to tech director John, as he asked if had gotten the prank on video. Of course, his hidden camera did just that, and in short order he had fleshed out the footage into a mini-movie called "Don't Mess With Fred." The district electrician gets credit for putting the elaborate trap together. I must say, I admire the teamwork and ingenuity. I can't imagine how disappointed everyone would have been if I had never touched the briefcase. Alas, it was bound to happen because my theory on humor is that something is funny as long as it continues to amuse me.

I'm getting ready to move away from some really great colleagues whom I have shared a lot of laughs and smiles with. The early indications are that my new locale will be fertile ground for laughs, though. I have already traded barbs about colleges, sports teams, and card playing; and I sincerely hope there are more to come.

Whoever coined the proverb, "Laughter is the best medicine," was on to something. The website www.helpguide.org states that laughter relaxes the whole body, boosts the immune system, triggers the release of endorphins, and protects the heart (by improving blood vessel function and increasing blood flow). Hey, who am I to argue?

I'm not some screwball who can't focus and doesn't take anything seriously. I just know life is short and should be enjoyed. Laughing with someone is good for the soul. The late, great poet Maya Angelou nailed it when she said, "I don't trust anyone who doesn't laugh" (www.psychologytoday.com/blog/living-the-questions/2013303/21-quotes-about-laughter).

I believe we are created to enjoy life, and I previously shared that I saw the joy of humor in my dad's life. As a teacher, I enjoyed being able to laugh with my students, and I know many sermons I have delivered have been enlivened with humorous illustrations. It's easier to learn when we're having fun. I know I'd rather be laughing when confronted with those moments when our only choice is to laugh or cry. There are physical, mental, and social benefits to laughter that I have just barely touched on here. I encourage you to seek out a good joke, a funny movie, or an amusing person today. Have a good laugh and enjoy the benefits!

Day 14:

Consider Carefully
How You Listen

I was reading Luke 7-8 this morning, and the text really spoke to me. These are familiar chapters of the Bible, presenting a high-speed montage of Jesus in action. John the Baptist sends men to ask if Jesus is really the one they have been waiting for, and Jesus tells them to go back and report what they have seen and heard.

There was a lot to see, without a doubt. Jesus healed many, forgave sins, cast out demons, and even brought people back to life from the dead! If one were observant, one would have seen women traveling with Jesus and the twelve disciples, helping to support them. We think of working women as ordinary, but these women were ahead of their time.

I know that I would have loved to <u>hear</u> the Master, too. I pay special attention to Jesus' words. Knowing this, the congregation I served thoughtfully gave me a "red letter" Bible that has all of Jesus' words in red. I look forward to using it. It could be the English teacher in me that appreciates Jesus' use of parables, which were very effective in connecting with the people. Jesus knew that those who were listening and <u>seeking</u>, those who really wanted to understand, would connect with the examples he used from everyday life. The Parable of the Sower, in Luke 8, is just that kind of story. However, Jesus had another reason for speaking in parables, and he shared it with His disciples, alluding to Isaiah 6:9: "but to others I speak in parables, so that 'though seeing, they may not see; though hearing, they may not understand'." (Luke 8:10, NIV)

Jesus knew the Pharisees and other religious leaders would not hear and understand. They would not listen and connect with the images He was sharing. They would be arrogant and dismissive until they perceived Him as a threat, and then they would seek to eliminate Him.

It is one of the tragedies of Biblical times that these devoutly religious people failed to understand that God was on Earth, walking in their midst. Unfortunately, there are plenty of judgmental, legalistic believers in the world today, too. Each of us should take a lesson from Jesus' words to the Pharisee whom He dined with. You might remember that this religious leader was critical of a sinful woman—and of Jesus for letting her anoint his feet with her tears and perfume. Jesus contrasts her attentiveness with Simon the Pharisee's indifference then says, "Therefore, I tell you, her many sins have been forgiven—for she loved much. But he who has been forgiven little loves little" (Luke 7:47, NIV).

That last statement, "But he who has been forgiven little loves little," cuts like a knife. Do you know self-righteous or self-important people who don't seem to have a gracious bone in their body? Do you know people who never seem thankful because they walk around in an aura of entitlement? I'm sure you do. There are plenty of people who have not acknowledged their own sinfulness, therefore being forgiven little and loving little. I am painfully aware of my sinful human nature and am very thankful that God redeemed me through Christ's sacrifice. I am a much better person in Christ, through the leading of the Spirit, than I ever could be on my own!

Even if you want to remove the Parable of the Sower from Luke 8 to a non-Biblical context, you can see the truth of the types of people Jesus displays. Let's have a quick recap of the parable first.

The Word of God is being compared to a farmer sowing seed:

1. Some fell on the path, was trampled, and was eaten by birds (like people who hear the Word, but the devil takes it away so that they can't hear and be saved).

2. Some fell on the rock, and the plants withered when they came up since they lacked moisture (like people who receive the Word with joy but have no root).

3. Some fell among thorns, which grew up with the plants and choked them (like people who hear but are choked by life's worries, riches, and pleasures).

4. Some fell on good soil and yielded a crop 100 times what was sown (like people with a noble and good heart who hear the word, retain it, and persevere) (Luke 8:5-15).

I don't know about you, but I don't get excited about a 75% failure rate. The Bible tells us, though, "The way is narrow" (Matthew 7:13). The world works against us having the right values. Christians are told that they are to be "in the world but not of the world" (Romans 12:2, John 15:19). I'm pretty sure you could apply this parable to people you work with or people you have met as well as to people who have heard the Word, inside or outside the church. Let me offer up an only slightly tongue-in-cheek example from the education world.

Let's presume that instead of the Word, what is being sown is quality professional development (If you are a cynical teacher reading this, suspend your disbelief please.):

1. Some teachers hear the information presented, but it falls on deaf ears because they have "been there, done that" and "this too shall pass."

2. Some teachers hear the information presented and are enthused about the possibilities, but they soon get busy and don't implement any strategies.

3. Some teachers hear the information presented and begin experimenting in their classes; but negative colleagues, questioning parents, and concern about time to plan make the effort too much to continue.

4. Some teachers hear the information presented, reflect on their practice, find some innovative and effective strategies that positively impact student learning, and share their successes and results with colleagues.

Now in case you think I'm ripping on 75% of teachers, understand that "hearing information presented" is not optimal professional development, and there does need to be adequate time for trial and error, collaboration, evaluation and adjustment of practice, etc. even with quality content. Far more than 25% of teachers would put professional development into practice given the chance, too. I used teacher professional development as an example because it is within my experience, but I bet you can think of better examples where people look but don't see and listen but don't hear.

Do you need more encouragement to "consider how carefully you listen"? Here are the next words of that verse: "Whoever has will be given more; whoever does not have, even what he thinks he has will be taken from him" (Luke 8:18). I can just hear some reactionaries screaming, "That's not fair!" I actually like the idea of a meritocracy somewhat. We all have to start somewhere, and we all have the opportunity to begin by being a good listener. Where we go from there really is somewhat up to us. If we continually try to understand and learn and turn our focus upon serving others, I firmly believe we will be in that group that is given more: more opportunity, more experience, more success, and more influence. There are relational and material rewards that are by-products of those things; but if we can stay focused on doing the right things rather than the rewards, then we will find peace and happiness.

God bless you and think about how well _you_ are listening! As the great John Wooden said, "It's what you learn after you know it all that counts."

Day 15:

Good-byes

I have been saying a lot of good-byes lately. Last night Packwood Christian Church had a going away party for Cindy and me. It was definitely bittersweet: it was great to get together and celebrate with people we know well and have worshipped with for more than 20 years in some cases, but it is sad to know we won't be there on a weekly basis anymore. Today is my last day in the office at Fairfield CSD. I have only worked for the district for five years, but Fairfield has been a very happy home for us. Cindy and I are moving away from an area where we have spent our whole adult working lives and married lives and where we have raised our sons. This is moving week, so things are hitting home. We have already had a litany of, "This is the last time I will do this," moments, and now the move is becoming very real.

I am ready for new challenges and opportunities, and I carry with me all of the wonderful relationships and experiences I have had throughout the last 24 years in this area. Good-byes are as natural as hellos, of course. Our older son doesn't live at home anymore. He has a successful career and a life of his own. Whether we are 90 minutes away or just across town from his apartment really is immaterial since he has a busy life anyway, and he's still just a text away. Our younger son has two more years of college, and our move will let us see more of him once summer is over. We are moving away from lots of friends and closer to other friends. Family will actually have an easier trip to come see us.

You can see the kind of internal dialogue we have been having with ourselves as we prepare for change. Especially in our hyper-connected electronic age, good-bye doesn't have to be so much of a good-bye. As I previously wrote when citing Ecclesiastes 3, there are different seasons in our lives, and God intends us to change and grow. I know that He will guide us and use us wherever we are.

Still, good-byes can be tough. The area I was least prepared for as a minister was officiating at funerals. I had the opportunity to preside at a dozen or so the last couple of years, some for people I knew and others for strangers. I use the word *opportunity* instead of something like *obligation* because I know that God has given me the chance to be a comforter and to share His promises. I always asked God to speak <u>to me</u> and <u>through me</u> and asked Him to provide to me the words that the family needed to hear. I have had a very good role model in Pastor Harlan "Frosty" Van Voorst, and I know God provided Frosty and his wife Eunice to our family and many others. I have also been that family member who needed comfort and was very thankful for Frosty and for Pastor Brian King as I said good-bye to my parents.

What I have come to realize is that good-byes aren't permanent, and we carry with us a piece of every person we have ever met. This has helped me to appreciate people and the power of relationships more. It has also made me more attentive to staying in touch with people and giving them my time.

Two things get in our way of really accepting changes and saying good-bye the right way: our selfish human nature and our linear view of time. Any believer knows that a fellow believer's passing is a joyous time. We typically call a funeral a *celebration of life*. We understand that our grief comes from a sense of loss. We focus on how we will miss our loved one. We wonder how we will ever adjust to life without the one we love. We have to consciously combat our self-centeredness to celebrate that the one who has left us in a physical sense has really gone home and is enjoying the blessing of eternal life with God! On an intellectual level, believers understand this, and once the raw emotion of a death passes, there is some truth to the old adage, "Time heals all wounds." Putting our linear view of time into perspective is much more daunting. We are so egotistical in thinking we can control the world with our Google calendars, cell phone alarms, and master plans! I am among the guiltiest. I always want to be early. I always want to know exactly when something is going to happen. I am impatient. I don't know how to relax. (My wife could have written those last four sentences. This tendency of mine is the bane of her existence. She is not wrapped quite as tightly as I am on this one issue. We complement each other well.).

If we can get outside of ourselves and attempt to see things through God's eyes, our perspective changes. That loved one we just lost—that is a soul harvest for God! That day that we just can't wait for—a thousand years is like a day to God! (2 Peter 3:8) An interesting, whimsical book I am reading right now, *Winter's Tale* by Mark Helprin, has a chapter titled "Nothing is Random." In it Helprin makes the point that although we view things as in motion, or underway, really everything is finished, and it is beautiful. That has to be the way God, the Alpha and Omega, Who spoke everything into existence, sees it. Helprin writes, "Time was invented because we cannot comprehend in one glance the enormous and detailed canvas that we have been given—so we track it, in linear fashion, piece by piece" (401). I find that incredibly insightful.

I am reminded of a line from John Gardner's *Grendel*, which I used to use as a companion piece while teaching *Beowulf* to high school seniors. *Grendel* is from the point-of-view of the monster that the Anglo-Saxon hero Beowulf defeats. As Grendel is in Beowulf's vise-like grip, having his arm torn off by the hero, he is trying to comprehend what is happening. He is enveloped in whirling colors and sounds and searing pain. Over and over the phrase "chewing the universe down to words" is used to describe Grendel's efforts to understand. I guess this is why I feel the need to write. I am trying to make sense of things. I am chewing the universe down to words.

I believe we do need to be thoughtful about things. When people have told me how helpful my first *40 Days* book was to them, I have felt very gratified. I hope this one is useful to people as well. We have to come to grips with our good-byes. I like the way that an aging Ulysses says it in the Alfred, Lord Tennyson poem of that name (See Appendix H): "I am a part of all that I have met." In the end Ulysses decides, "Tis not too late to seek a newer world." He determines "to strive, to seek, to find, and not to yield."

May you carry your yesterdays with you as you seek new tomorrows, and may you have a sense that all of it—yesterday, today, and tomorrow—is a part of one glorious whole that God has already created. Bless you!

Day 16:

Stories

We all love stories, and we all have them. In the days of Oral Tradition, long before the electronic age, storytellers were revered; and they were the chief source of entertainment. Obviously we have a lot of different kinds of entertainment available to us today, but everyone still enjoys a good story no matter what medium it comes in (book, newspaper, eBook, TV, movie, Facebook, YouTube, you name it).

It is worth noting that the best stuff of stories, at least if we are talking about personal narratives, comes from situations that are disconcerting, inconveniencing, or downright exasperating. There's a lot of truth to that old expression, "I don't know whether to laugh or cry," uttered from the midst of these moments. Of course, these trials are often quite humorous once we have a little time and distance from them. I really believe that the better we get at quickly recognizing the humor and absurdity of the situations we find ourselves caught in, the more adept we become at appreciating and sharing what makes a good story and the more we enjoy life.

I'm sure most of us have a good travel story. As I write, I am just a couple of days removed from one of ours. We began a trip home from Boston the afternoon of July 2, intending to arrive at the home we have just moved into that evening so that we could continue unpacking and I could get into my new office the morning of July 3. We were flying a carrier we have vowed to never use again after a chaotic trip fifteen years ago; the trip out to Boston had gone deceptively well, though.

The trouble began at Gate A17. We were there plenty early for our 4:00 P.M. departure, even after killing a little time with a Fuddruckers burger. A mechanical problem introduced a thirty-minute delay, quickly followed by a second delay. Suddenly our connection in Atlanta was in question. The agent at the gate was doing her best to work miracles, probably due to her professionalism and friendliness, although she made a point of mentioning that her husband was named Arthur, just as I am. There was another Arthur on the move that afternoon, trying to decide whether he was content being a tropical storm or aspired to be a hurricane. More about Arthur later.

Arthur's wife, the airport employee, kept our original flight in place (even though it was obvious we were going to miss the connection), got us on standby for a flight to Detroit that would get us to Des Moines earlier than our original itinerary, and booked an insurance flight to Chicago that would then take us to Des Moines with a midnight arrival. It was confirmed. We would get home that night, one way or another. Ri-i-i-i-i-i-ght.

We went to gate A20 to monitor our standby status. That flight was delayed twice also. There was little margin for error to make the connection in Detroit, so of course we made the flight and took the risk. We checked our bags through to Des Moines so that we could run faster to our connecting flight. We would have half an hour or less if all went well. Enter Arthur.

We sat on the tarmac in Boston for two hours while the pilots talked with people about a way around the storm (first a northern route and then a southern one), calculated how much fuel we had, and repeatedly tried to file their flight plan with the tower (at the exact same time every other similarly delayed plane was peppering the controller with requests). At one point passengers who preferred to stay in Boston that night instead of Detroit were allowed to deplane, once it was clear all connections would be missed. For the record, Detroit to Des Moines took off and arrived ahead of schedule. We decided to stick it out and get one leg of the return trip knocked out. We'd always heard Detroit was beautiful in July, and we were seated in an Exit aisle (Ah, the space).

At some point we got airborne, flew for an hour or so then heard the captain say that we were back over Boston after re-routing. Right around that time I gave passing consideration to the flight attendant's offer to make my bloody Mary mix order an actual bloody Mary at no charge. We arrived at Detroit around 10:00 P.M. (two hours after our connection), and the re-booking line was not a happy place. I chose to scan my boarding pass on my own for our re-booked morning flight and accepted a voucher for a reduced rate hotel rather than waiting in line to harangue airline employees, which was the more popular choice among passengers.

After a protracted shuttle ride with two other stops before our hotel, we arrived at what the kind, foreign-sounding man on the phone had described as "the cheapest, closest hotel." The young man at the counter muttered, "I hate _____(mentally insert airline name)," as he tried to handle a spate of displaced travelers checking in, answered the phone, and dispensed shuttle and breakfast information. He did inform us that our room key entitled us to a 10% discount at the restaurant next door; and when he was caught up later, I bothered him for some tooth-brushes and toothpaste. You remember we had checked our bags through to Des Moines, right?

After an 11:00 P.M. dinner— I had a cold tuna melt and cold French fries— that was far from perfect but tasted okay, we returned to our dusty, retro 1970ish room for a short night's sleep.

The next morning we caught a shuttle to the airport and listened to the driver scream at someone in a foreign language on his cell phone for the entire ride to the terminal. We sailed through security and got to our gate. I had a decent cup of regular coffee when the barista told me the latte machine was down. We boarded on time and settled in on a less than capacity flight. Life was good.

Prior to take off we noticed the lone flight attendant appeared upset, and not long afterward a uniformed police officer darkened the door of the small jet. He removed a lady from the front row. She went peaceably with the officer. We estimated that she was in her seventies, based on the very frail ninety-something woman, probably her mom, whom she had brought on with her in a wheel chair. An EMT had to help that lady off. The airline staff apologized profusely for the delay (something they must spend a lot of time perfecting in air travel school). The pilot said it was his call to remove the lady, who was "having a bad day." The flight attendant said, "We have to take all threatening language seriously." The rest of the flight was uneventful, with me sprawling into the aisle (I had some unfolding to do after contorting myself and leaning over sideways in basically a crawl space to use the bathroom on the plane—it's really tough to just relax and go in that position.) and Cindy resting comfortably with the portly gentleman in front of her reclining his seat into her legs.

Upon landing, we found our luggage right away, and a friend pulled up to pick us up right after we walked outside. We were thankful that she had taken a break from studying for her driver's test to get us and happy that she was willing to drive with a license that had expired in December.

The next day truly felt like Independence Day after being delivered from that trip, and that evening we were on the back porch of our chauffeur friend's house with her husband, several others, and her. We were there to watch fireworks, and for the first half an hour, we were pretty sure we were missing the show due to a couple of evergreens that had had a really good growth year. Every now and then we could catch a little glimpse of color. Those of us who had the right angle were enjoying the display of a small town about twelve miles away. Eventually, there were some local fireworks seen, but I have to say that joking about the pre-show/possible no-show was more fun than the show itself.

I have written the bulk of this entry on the deck behind our new house, listening to a cacophony of blackbirds that crap like elephants on our driveway but thankfully not yet on me. I have to tell you, I am truly thankful for the crazy things life throws at us. Every bump in the road provides fodder for the next story (Maybe I'll tell you about the pontoon boat some of our admin team got stuck on sometime). I hope you take the time to share and preserve these stories. Life really is funny. Take a few minutes and write or record one of your own travel adventures today!

Day 17:

Brothers

Events have conspired to make me nostalgic today. At Village Inn I enjoyed watching and eavesdropping upon a family with three young boys this morning, and as I listened to the mom explain second hand smoke to her boys and urge patience when the pancakes were delivered without chocolate chips, I remembered how much fun it was to raise our sons. They are great brothers to each other, and I am really glad they got to experience having brothers. Tonight my older brother called to catch up, and he is the father of two sons, too. That's a neat thing we share. Later tonight, I'm going to give my little brother a call. He's 43 now but forever my "little brother" (Hi, Robin).

As I was growing up, I know I watched my older brother closely, and I always wanted to do whatever he did just a little sooner or just a little better than he did. It was the same way with our boys. Of course, every child is different and no little brother surpasses his big brother in everything. The effort makes for a lot of sibling rivalry, but fortunately it's not usually a Cain and Abel sequel. In fact, there's a magical moment in there somewhere when big brother becomes a great cheerleader and supporter for little brother, and little brother comes to respect and revere big brother. I am very happy that our sons love and support each other and make no secret of it.

It took a while to get to that point. Our sons are 3-1/2 years apart in age, which is just close enough to be dangerous. Jordan had Trey by the throat more than a few times growing up, and Trey got very skilled at bending Jordan's fingers back to secure his release. My older brother Ed was good at chucking the basketball at his cocky, smart-mouthed younger brother Art, and my younger brother Robin learned that a well-timed sneak attack evened the score for a lot of bullying. I think I still ache from one time he dropped his considerable bulk on my back as I lay relaxing, watching TV on the living room floor. I also remember him popping me in the mouth as we traveled down the road in the back seat, and then using our mom as a shield.

Sometimes we were forced to collaborate, like the time I pushed Robin into the cast iron stove, sending the top of it through a curved glass china. I know my parents didn't believe he "bumped" it while hopping up off the couch to go to the kitchen during a commercial, but we kept a united front and stuck to the story. I'm pretty sure their last words to us before they left that night were, "Don't fight." It's unbelievable how many antiques my siblings and I broke when we were growing up!

There are definitely different seasons to siblinghood. One day I'm talking my little brother into a fun game when we take turns hitting the little red rubber ball, attached by a rubber band to the wooden paddle, at each other (a task that he was way too uncoordinated to successfully accomplish at the time), and the next day he's too big to pick on without incurring some serious injury myself. I'm glad there are different seasons to siblinghood. I enjoy the boys supporting each other way more than I did the public fights in grocery stores or on college visits; and now that my wife's brother is 40, he hardly ever bugs her by making annoying noises.

I get nostalgic more often these days, now that Cindy and I are "empty nesters." I wouldn't trade parenthood for anything, though, and I hope my parents had the same joy raising my siblings and me. I know they were proud of their three sons, daughter, and adopted son. They were wonderful grandparents, too, and I hope I get to experience that as well.

Obviously there are families that aren't close and siblings that have had rifts occur. My prayer for them is that they find a way to reconnect and reconcile. Life is too short to miss out on the blessings of family. Take a minute today and think about one of those great times you had with a brother or other family member. Then pick up your phone or get on Facebook and ask them, "Hey, do you remember when we. . .?" You won't regret it. Enjoy your family!

Day 18:

Competition

It's World Cup time and NBA free agency (not to mention a lively local debate about conference affiliation), and I have been thinking quite a bit about competition lately. I have often prided myself on being a competitor, and I have even described myself as *hyper-competitive* as if that is a good thing. I was the dad who wasn't going to just let his kids win the game. I might have created a monster there. I remember one of our kids tore up the plum card in Candy-land because he didn't want to get sent back to the start on the board. Since this is true confessions time, I will admit, I still struggle with wanting to have the last word or with thinking I'm always right.

I think there are definite benefits to competition. Competition drives us to be our best. Competition gives a nod to meritocracy: if you're more talented, you will likely win. Competition can humble us, too, and teach us perseverance. Even though I don't really golf competitively, that game keeps me humble and hungry to get better. Compete enough against good competition and you find out that there's usually someone who is just a little better than you out there.

Even though I still very much like to win and I still really enjoy the competition, whether it's a game of cards with friends or a free throw contest with my son, I have learned some things about competition. One thing I learned is that losing is rarely fatal, and as cliché as it is, we can learn from losses. We could probably play it safe in life and avoid some losses and heartache, but I believe we know the risks of that: "Nothing ventured, nothing gained," (which dictionary. com says has been around as a similar expression since the late 1300s) and " 'Tis better to have loved and lost than never to have loved at all," (wisdom from poet Alfred Lord Tennyson). These old adages illuminate the possible cost of playing it safe. Perhaps the most important thing I have learned about competition is that it's not about <u>comparing</u>.

I really admire the work and life of the late, great Coach John Wooden. Wooden consistently emphasized with his teams that they were really in competition with <u>themselves</u>, striving to be the best <u>they</u> could be. He convinced them—and his teams' success bears this out—that if they focused on their own conditioning and skills and were driven to be their personal best, then they didn't have to worry about their opponent. Winning would take care of itself. Coach Wooden didn't talk about winning with his teams. Can you imagine that from a coach whose teams won <u>seven straight</u> NCAA men's basketball titles (ten overall)? This idea didn't originate with Wooden. I ran across a quote by the great American novelist William Faulkner. Jim Collins used this quote in his excellent book *Built to Last*. Faulkner advised,

"Don't bother just to be better than your contemporaries or predecessors. Try to be better than yourself." That is the essence of competition and improvement that Wooden grasped.

This wasn't a gimmick for Wooden. It's who he was. He was crystal clear on his values, which were well represented in his Pyramid of Success. The Hall of Fame coach included a definition of *success* with his pyramid. Wooden wrote, "Success is peace of mind which is a direct result of self-satisfaction in knowing you did your best to become the best that you are capable of becoming." Do you see how this definition informed Wooden's view of competition and how it led to incredible focus and freedom for his players?

Let's talk about focus for a minute. Typically, a more focused competitor is a more effective competitor. Wooden's teams were focused on one thing: being their best. That kept them out of the comparison trap. That kept them in a growth mindset. That put them in charge of their own destiny to a large degree. Wooden took this idea to the extreme; he didn't just give it lip service as a coach. For example, Wooden didn't scout opponents. He didn't worry about what the other team was going to do. He focused on what his team needed to do. I'm sure anyone who has coached can argue for the necessity of scouting, but no one can argue with Wooden's results.

Ask yourself this: wouldn't it be liberating not to have to worry about measuring up to an external standard? Would you enjoy just being able to be yourself and do your best? I hope many people reading this book live their lives that way, and if one's personal standards are high enough, I think one can come close. I suppose there are some assumptions I am making here that impact one's ability to live this way and be successful. These assumptions would include things like the following:

1. You are willing to work hard and do a good job.

2. You like things you put your name on to be done well.

3. You believe you should always be striving to be better, more knowledgeable, more effective, more loving people.

4. You accept where you and others are at, but you don't expect yourself and others to stay there.

These assumptions capture the true essence of competition, I believe. #1 reminds me of an old Theodore Roosevelt quote I love: "Far and away the best life has to offer is to work hard at work worth doing." #2 reminds me of wisdom from Aristotle: "We are what we repeatedly do. Excellence, then, is not an act but a habit." I believe both of these quotes appeared on Iowa High School Athletic Association posters years ago. #3 reminds me of our stewardship responsibilities. I believe we are created in God's image, with a soul and a spark of the divine in us. Striving to be better in all aspects of our lives (the highest form of competition, in my opinion) is our responsibility. Every person has been given certain gifts, and we should develop them. I firmly believe that if we focus on being our best and serving others, *success* will take care of itself. I know a lot of people chase after things—visible, material signs that they have succeeded. Their competition is in amassing more or doing better than others. Remember Wooden's description of success, though. It starts off with "peace of mind." Can we really ask for more than that?

I understand that there is a popular culture and an advertising industry that do not champion Wooden's simple definition. I also accept that as humans we constantly judge others and draw conclusions, often erroneous, about their happiness and success. Be careful of doing that. We don't always know what others are thinking or experiencing. Read the old poem "Richard Cory" (See Appendix I) for a stark reminder of that (I wrote this entry a few weeks before the suicide of Robin Williams, a real-life reminder of this same truth).

I enjoy competition. I have a little bit of a Type A personality. I have learned not to take myself too seriously, though, and I no longer believe that "win at all costs" is a good way to live. I like to think this is wisdom I have gained in my life and not merely a result of being a long-suffering Cubs fan. Take just a minute and think about these questions today:

1. Am I a competitive person?
2. What does it mean to be competitive?
3. Do I have a growth mindset?
4. Is it more satisfying to me to do a good job or to beat someone else?
5. What things do I need to do to consider myself a winner?

Play hard, have fun, and strive to do your best!

Day 19:
Confidence and Humility

I have thought quite a bit about confidence and humility, and I know that they are not opposites as some people might think. As a young adult I projected outward confidence while possessing inward humility, but not of the healthy kind. My outward confidence was based on my abilities, what I knew I could <u>do</u> or accomplish. My inward humility was bathed in uncertainty, not knowing who I was and not liking myself very well. Sometimes both the outward confidence and inward humility were fueled by alcohol or reckless behavior. At the time I knew this wasn't the best life had to offer, and I believe now that God doesn't intend His children to feel the way I did sometimes. I found myself needing peace, and I envied people who seemed at ease with themselves.

I should note that I got very good grades and achieved quite a few successes during this time. There were plenty of high notes, and I wasn't sitting in a dark room feeling depressed. I had been raised right and had decent values. However, I did not really understand confidence and humility, and I know that not being very happy with myself sometimes led to my not treating others as I should.

Over time I have realized that I had things backwards. What we need is <u>inward confidence</u> and <u>outward humility</u>, not the other way around. My inward confidence today comes from trusting God, knowing my priorities, and counting my blessings.

I believe there is a God and that He created the universe and each individual with a purpose. I study His Word and believe His promises. He knit me together in my mother's womb (Psalm 139:13), has plans to prosper me (Jeremiah 29:11), and has redeemed me for eternal life with Him (Hebrews 9:12 and other verses). As a result, I have nothing to fear. I know what my priorities are. I call them my *Big Rocks*: faith, family, and work. I have been richly blessed in all of these areas, and I am thankful. God has given me the peace that passes human understanding (Philippians 4:7).

This kind of inner confidence makes it natural to project an outward humility. I am very confident that I will be successful when acting in accordance with God's Will for my life. The focus is not on me and what I can <u>do</u> but on who I <u>am</u> and how I can serve others and share God's love.

I believe God intends it this way. All of those people striving to achieve their goals (exactly the kind of person I was for years) place their trust in their own ability and work ethic. Many of them become successful by the world's standards. Uncommon success comes when a person trusts in God, turns his eyes upon Jesus, and answers the call to serve. Just being willing to serve, saying, "yes" when asked, has led to many opportunities and joys in my life. Answering the call, like Jesus' first disciples did, can be daunting but so rewarding.

Focus on who you are, not what you can do. Strive to be a good person, not a successful or powerful one. That's what the Biblical King Solomon did. He prayed for and received discernment to lead his people; then God gave him great material success, too. If you find yourself seeking things that are good but aren't the most important things, do a little priority check on yourself. The Bible says, "Seek ye first the kingdom of God, and His righteousness; and all these things shall be added unto you" (Matthew 6:33, KJV). "Ask and it will be given to you; seek and you will find; knock and the door will be opened to you" (Luke 11:9, NIV). But remember, Jesus stands at the door and knocks, too (Revelation 3:20). If you let him into your heart and begin to experience His joy, you will be filled with an inner confidence based in trust in His Word and power. If you have this inner confidence and have defeated the demons that commonly plague people: insecurity, greed, self-centeredness, dishonesty, substance abuse, etc., then you are able to go out into the world as a servant, projecting humility and love.

This humility is not a false humility, being disingenuous to seek praise, for example. True humility is the outward expression of your inward confidence, knowing, as Paul famously wrote, "I can do all things through Christ, who strengthens me" (Philippians 4:13, NKJV). You place your confidence in God, letting Him work through you and empower you. If you allow God to use you, He can accomplish more than you dreamed.

I know that I am a much better man with God in my life than I would be without Him. My faith, family, and work—my Big Rocks—are the focal points through which He works. Left to my own devices, I can only go as far as my talents and energy can take me. On my own I get sidetracked and lose my orientation of inward confidence/ outward humility. I recently received a compliment from a person who told me I was a great leader and a genuine person. That's God working in my life, giving me inward confidence and outward humility. That's the heart of servant leadership. If you haven't thought about these things much before, I pray you will pause and do so today. What is getting in the way of your being at peace and feeling inward confidence? In your relationships with others, are you able to see that it's not about you? Pray to God for help. Let me offer a little prayer for us both here:

Dear God,

We want to feel Your peace. We want to go through life confident in You and humble in our dealings with others. Use us as instruments of Your love and grace and bless our families and us. In Jesus' name we pray,

Amen.

Day 20:
Deprivation (but not really)

Not too long ago I read Malcolm Gladwell's *Outliers*, which really forces a person to consider cultural forces at work in people's lives and how those forces shape people. Gladwell went so far as to identify the perfect year and ethnicity to be a successful lawyer or the perfect time and conditions to be an influential software engineer, for example. He said the romanticized rags-to-riches stories of how someone made it big in spite of disadvantages are wrong. Research shows that person made it big <u>because of</u> so-called disadvantages. The English proverb, "Necessity is the mother of invention," comes to mind. I am following up Gladwell's book with Rich Cohen's *Monsters: The 1985 Chicago Bears and the Wild Heart of Football*. In that book the legendary Bears coach, "Iron Mike" Ditka shares a similar example, discussing why great quarterbacks (e.g. Unitas, Montana, Marino, Namath) have been spawned by western Pennsylvania: "It's the work ethic, the way people were brought up. The parents came from the old country and worked in the mills and mines. People didn't have anything but didn't need anything" (98). That sounds like deprivation to me, but not really, since it paid so many dividends.

What brought this weighty topic to mind were the "woe is me" tales of my youth, which I know I have regaled my wife and sons with. Recently I realized I must have shared more widely since a friend of mine brought up one of my Horatio Alger-like examples in casual conversation one night. The memory in question dates back to 1974 or so, when I was the tender age of eight, just old enough for style to matter to kids.

I grew up in Northern Iowa, home of cold winters and snow forts. Kids needed gloves. I remembered having those thin brown work gloves, which were soaked through in a second; that was fine with me. What I am forever scarred by is another model my mother gave me to wear to school one day: Handy Ann gardening gloves. I'm sure these were the only gloves to be found in the house, but holy cow! These were white women's work gloves adorned with colorful pictures of a smiling little blond girl who looked like Little Red Riding Hood. In case there was any doubt about the femininity of this accoutrement, the words "Handy Ann" were plastered all over the gloves. All I can say is, "Thank you, Mom, for teaching me to be tough." I am sitting here thinking of Johnny Cash's "A Boy Named Sue." (By the way, being named "Art," or more properly, "Arthur Meryl," has its own set of challenges for a young boy.)

I know my wife would not have sent our boys to school in those gloves, and they would have rebelled if we had tried. To be fair, we were a family of four kids plus frequent foster children, getting by on my dad's teacher salary. We didn't have a lot of frills. We shared rooms. We ate a lot of goulash. If we ate at the café across the street, my choices were grilled cheese or egg sandwich, and I would be drinking water. My mom was a practical, hard-working woman who was an older sibling raised on a dairy farm without a lot of luxuries, too. "You need some gloves? Here you go."

Which brings me to my boots. All I wanted was some of those cool, green rubber boots like most kids had. I played with G.I. Joes like most boys of my generation, and those boots evoked manly adventures. I never did get those boots. I got the black rubber, zip-over-your-shoes, old man boots like the old man who was always out shoveling in *Home Alone* wore. I assume mine were handed down. I think they were too big. I remember a procedure involving empty bread wrappers and culminating in wet socks and cold feet after coming in from a snowy recess. In fifth grade it was a continual challenge to elude the recess monitors and get out of the building in just my tennis shoes (Pro-keds and not Jordans or the 70s equivalent undoubtedly). The rest I have blocked from my memory.

I learned to ride a bike on something Mike and Frank, the American Pickers, would probably rave about and pay a couple of hundred bucks for, a bonafide antique, a boxy tank of a dented relic that must have weighed 200 pounds. No wonder I was a late learner. I know my older brother and sister both learned on that old orange bike, too. I always wanted a ten-speed. I never got one, but I was pretty excited by the dark green three-speed I got for one birthday, and I bet it was somewhat of a sacrifice for my parents.

I rode the heck out of that thing, slipping down to the Pop Shoppe for an arcade game and cream soda whenever I had a few extra bucks from my dishwashing job. Unfortunately, this match made in heaven ended badly. Flying down the big hill on Washington Avenue, the main downtown thoroughfare of Iowa Falls, I hit a rock and the front wheel flew off my bike. I flew before Michael Jordan even thought of it. I was airborne forever, and you know what they say: "It's not the fall that gets you; it's the landing." I came to earth in a friction-laden skid that left me skinned and bleeding from ankle to shoulder on my ride side. I came to rest in the entry to Kum and Go with my twisted bike beside me. This was an epic fail that would absolutely blow up on YouTube today. I wouldn't see carnage like that until many years later, when our younger son ran over our older son's friend with a four-wheeler in a gravel driveway. The friend had a Supersoaker and zigged while Trey zagged at about 30 MPH. I think the friend, now 24, is still picking gravel out of his body. His dad and I were supervising, loosely speaking, while playing Risk inside.

Somehow, a couple of years after my three-speed, I got a moped. Friends had some cool ones, stylish red mopeds that topped out at about 40-45 MPH. I had a used yellow 1971 Honda Express that went 32 on a flat road on a good day. Except for being a big, gawky teen that looked like Runaway Ralph in my red helmet, I was content. I did, however, drive like a complete idiot. Once I hit a curb going full speed and went flying, bouncing my chin off the pavement when I landed. I was on the other side of town and drove home bleeding profusely. I tried to sneak into the house in my bloody shirt to assess the damage without my parents knowing, but my mom saw me and deadpanned in her classic understated way, "I think you may need a stitch." I got six and still have the scar on my chin. That was my second worst moped accident.

"The worst?" you ask. That would be the time I exited the four lanes at max speed to go jump the large dirt hill out by River Hills Mall. It was great for a second as I flew high in the air. I sensed there was a problem as I performed what BMX riders refer to as a "Superman." The moped was out in front of me. I was stretched out behind it, holding onto to the handgrips. When I came to earth, my adolescent manhood led the way, making some very solid contact with the gas tank. Oh, my. Thank you, God, for making that sickening pain brief and for allowing me to father children.

I would love to rattle on with stories of misadventures with my first two cars, a 1972 Caprice Classic Woody station wagon, nicknamed the "Death Mobile" by friends since the wired up muffler pointed into the partially stuck open automatic rear window, and a 1973 yellow and black Maverick Grabber that was my older brother's first car. The Grabber had no power steering, brakes, locks, or windows and no A/C; but it did have AM radio and genuine brown vinyl seats. Those suckers were hot in the summer sun!

I have to say, what we <u>don't</u> have is pretty important sometimes. It makes us appreciate what we do have. It teaches us to delay gratification and to work hard and sacrifice. I have been smiling the whole time I have been writing this. Maybe that's masochistic, but I'm thankful I learned to work for things and that I've taken a few lumps along the way. It was a <u>big deal</u> when I bought my first pair of leather Converse basketball shoes for $45 in ninth grade. I had played (and even run 7th grade track) in good old canvas Chuck Taylors to that point. I had a stylish navy blue pair I bought for $6 at Ridiculous Days and wore to camp about 18 years before that was in style. I took some crap, but that seemed to let up when I took it to people on the court.

Most of us probably have some of these "walked uphill both ways to school" stories in our arsenal, and we have an obligation to share them with our kids. Everyone is much better off for having experienced some deprivation. And, yes, I understand that I am not writing about the real deprivation that truly needy people face all over the world. When we don't have everything we'd like, we learn to appreciate what we have. I hope that never changes. I could carry this right on to discuss places we've lived, vehicles we've lacked, beds we've slept in, etc. in our early married life especially. We weren't really deprived, but those days make us appreciate today's comforts more. We do realize there are much more important things than material comforts in life. I always liked O. Henry's story "The Gift of the Magi" as an illustration of that. I hope we never fail to appreciate the blessings in our lives, understanding that we probably won't ever have everything we want. In the words of those great philosophers, the Rolling Stones, " You can't always get what you want, but if you try sometime, you find you get what you need!"

Best wishes to you for a little deprivation! Take a minute and reflect about some times when "doing without" really proved to be a blessing.

Day 21:

Empathy

My entire adult working life I have been blessed to have work that requires working with people. This truly is a blessing because, as I often note, I have no skills, and I am the least mechanical person you know. I also feel, at times, that my body is falling apart, making me unfit for sustained physical labor. Just what does that leave for me to do? Using my head, working with people, solving problems, coaching and encouraging, providing ethical leadership, planning, evaluating, and communicating are the basic remaining skills. An important one to add to those is caring, and caring cannot be accomplished without empathy.

Much of the work I have done as a teacher, coach, school administrator, and pastor the last 26+ years has been about discerning and overcoming challenges that people face. When it comes to other human beings, unless we have very similar backgrounds and similar challenges and triumphs in our lives, we have to have empathy to discern human needs. For example, I know that having to sit on the bench as a reserve my last two years of college basketball as I struggled through serious injuries made me more empathetic to injured players when I was a coach. Throughout high school and my first two years of college I pretty much "starred," meaning I got to be in the action and only had to sit if it was a blowout or if I was in foul trouble. Coaches expect role players, those with less than a starring or starting role, to be as enthusiastic or more enthusiastic than the players getting lots of minutes. It's their role to be spark plugs and cheerleaders. I believe this, too, but it's tough sitting on the bench, and being hurt helped me experience and understand that.

Playing time is not a life and death matter, but empathy is more beneficial than sympathy when there is a death of a loved one. I will issue one caution, though. Nobody who is grieving needs to hear, "I know just how you feel," or "It must have been God's Will." Even empathy has its limits. No one knows <u>just</u> how someone else feels in that situation. People handle grief and loss differently, no matter how applicable the "Six Stages of Loss" or other models might be. <u>And</u> no one can fully know the Will of God. Plenty of things happen in the world—because of free will, sin, natural disasters, and disease—that God isn't sitting in Heaven smiling about and putting His stamp of approval on.

Though I would have preferred that my parents passed peacefully in their sleep together when they were 98 and 100 instead of in a car wreck at age 59 and wheel-chair-bound and cancer-ridden at age 65, their deaths shaped and informed me in many ways. My personal grieving process was somewhat stoic acceptance, followed by intermittent emotional attacks that seemed to come out of nowhere.

Four months after Dad's death I was watching *The Patriot* in a theatre in Ireland with Cindy and a girls' basketball team. The father-son theme in this Mel Gibson movie is strong, and it made me a blubbering idiot. Mother's Day and Father's Day are bittersweet, as are Palm Sunday (when my dad died and mom was paralyzed) and Christmas break (Mom died December 21, and we had her funeral December 26).

I have moved past grief, though, to feel my parents' presence in my life more powerfully than ever before. They are present in who I am, what I believe, and everything I do. This is the hope I share with people who are dealing with loss. It's not quite as simple as, "Time heals all wounds," but there is hope. When we are dealing with death and when we are going through our daily lives, we need to stay focused on the essentials, which I call the Big Rocks. As I frequently state, my Big Rocks are faith, family, and work. I try not to impose my values on others, but keeping the focus on those things helps me handle life's ups and downs. My typical prayer for someone in mourning is that he/she finds comfort in faith, family, and good memories of the departed loved one. My own experience helps me empathize and offer hope to others.

In my work I often have to navigate complex issues and differences of opinion. Each situation is unique, but all of them have something in common: they involve humans. Remembering that God made every single one of us unique, with our own foibles and idiosyncrasies, helps me to practice empathy. If we can get to the point where we get past sitting in judgment (a tall order—I catch myself doing it a lot), then we can understand the other person even if we don't necessarily agree with the other person. I can tell you from experience that oftentimes people just want to know they have been heard. Guns 'N Roses sang, "We all just need a little patience." I would tweak that just a little and say, "We all just need some understanding."

In order to understand, one obviously has to be able to listen. There is no empathy without listening. You've heard the saying, "God gave us two ears and one mouth for a reason." I have cited Covey's habit many times: "Seek first to understand, then to be understood." *Fierce Conversations* training teaches that a coaching conversation should be about 80% listening and 20% speaking. Communication experts teach *active listening*, which involves paraphrasing what one has heard to ensure clarity and understanding: "So, what I think I heard you say is …" Effective sales-people will mimic the style, cadence, and language of a prospective buyer to make the customer feel comfortable and increase the likelihood of a sale. I understand that these examples might seem manipulative or artificial. The goal is to have these communication skills become a natural part of how we listen and talk with others. The advice, "Fake it 'til you make it," comes to mind. That might sound cynical, but it is important to play the part, to act as though you <u>are</u> in order to <u>become</u>.

If you are not yet an empathetic person, you can practice becoming one. When you ask someone, "How are you?" try really listening to his/her answer. Don't ask it if you don't want to know. Learn to listen to really understand rather than plotting what you are going to say next. Connect to the person you are speaking to right where he/she is, in the circumstances he/she faces. You know the old advice: "Put yourself in their shoes." In the end you don't have to <u>be</u> them, and you don't even have to agree with them. You just have to come to an understanding. Worst case, it can be "agree to disagree," doing so respectfully.

If you don't know if you are an empathetic person, just ask. Probably a poker-playing truism applies here: "If you don't know who the fish in the game is, you're the fish." In this application, "If you don't know if you're an empathetic person, you're probably not." There are a lot of people out there who are painfully unaware of self because taking time to reflect can be tough. If you have a trusted accountability partner, ask him/her straight out, "Do you think I am an empathetic person? Can I relate to people who are struggling?" Once they stop looking at you like you have two heads, they will probably give you some good insight.

If you are in a leadership position, I sincerely encourage you to provide anonymous evaluation, or survey, opportunities to those you serve. I was giving all students an opportunity to evaluate my class and me anonymously 26 years ago, long before every oil change, hotel stay, and airline flight resulted in a customer service survey. There's a reason everyone is doing this: feedback matters. I continued anonymous feedback as a principal and superintendent. In my new position all 450 employees of the district will be invited to anonymously evaluate me and offer comments, and I will share evaluation data with the board. Some people are reluctant to do this, but I feel that discontent is better voiced than driven underground if it exists. We can learn from our critics, too, you know.

Is there a risk in doing this? It depends on how secure you are in what you are doing. Because I feel I have the right values and work hard to live those values, I'm not overly threatened. I try to have empathy with and express appreciation for every person in the organization. If I'm coming up short, the anonymous evaluation might let me know. Appreciation is expressed through that vehicle, too, usually way more appreciation than complaint.

I am a tremendous believer in stewardship and continuous improvement. I know there is always room for us to be kinder, more loving, and more supportive. Empathy is the key for us to begin that growth in ourselves. I like the thought, "If you want to change the world, start with yourself." Gandhi said it a little more poetically: "Be the change you want to see in the world."

What people in your life could use a little understanding right now? Who are you struggling to connect with? List some people you will go seek empathy with:

1.

2.

3.

4.

5.

em•pa•thy **noun** \ 'em-pa-thē\

: the feeling that you understand and share another person's experiences and emotions: the ability to share someone else's feeling

(www.merriam-webster.com)

Day 22:
Happy Gilmore, Tommy Boy, and Ty Webb

It's a lazy Sunday afternoon, and my wife is lying on the couch, looking at me with a bemused expression. She must have thought I looked a little crazed as I searched for a notepad. "What are you doing, writing Day 22?" she asked as I told her I was searching for paper. "Why, yes, I am." And I'm drawing on Adam Sandler's Happy Gilmore, Chris Farley's Tommy Boy, and Chevy Chase's Ty Webb for inspiration. I am tapping into these paragons of excellence partly because they're so darned much fun and partly because I like the challenge of having a serious conversation about life, using these goofballs as examples. So what can we learn from Happy Gimlore, Tommy Boy, and Ty Webb? How about the following: 1. Be yourself. 2. Have fun. 3. Accept challenges. 4. Find your way.

Be yourself is a very easy lesson to glean from these sophomoric cinematic stars. Happy Gilmore is an erstwhile hockey player, forced to take up golf to save his grandma's house from foreclosure. I can say with certainty that I would watch a lot more televised golf if Happy Gilmore were on the PGA Tour. He takes the stodgy tour by storm, imploring the gallery, "Let's make a little noise here, huh!" as he prepares to launch a slap shot-style drive. A female golf executive, destined to become a love interest, sees a diamond in the rough and calls Happy, "a colorful, emotional, working class hero." Happy is a work boot-wearing man of the people, unlike the tour leader, Shooter McGavin. Happy knows no pretentiousness; he's "happy" to pick up a homeless guy as his caddy. Tommy Boy is one of a kind, too. He is genuine and lovable, fun loving and loyal. Unfortunately, he's a seemingly incurable screw up, too. David Spade's character is sent out to mentor/babysit Tommy on a cross-country sales trip that holds the fate of the company. Of course, there are challenges and near disasters, but through it all, Tommy Boy is sincere and genuine. In the end you can't help but love him. To be honest, in real life there are very few people I don't really like no matter what their views or personalities, as long as they are genuine. I would have to say I share Holden Caulfield's views on this. He's the protagonist of Salinger's *The Catcher in the Rye*, and he rails against phonies more than anything else. Tommy Boy is the genuine article. So is *Caddyshack* character Ty Webb. Ty seems totally unconcerned with other people's expectations for him. He is supremely talented, and some would say he is squandering his talent. Ty Webb is unfazed by his talent and celebrity. He is not above befriending an up and coming caddy, and he has huge checks lying un-cashed in his cluttered abode. He's his own guy, and it fits him well. Naturally these movie characters aren't intended to be role models, but we should strive to be as comfortable in our own skins and as genuine as they are.

When we are comfortable with ourselves, it is a lot more natural to *have some fun*. For Happy Gilmore fun is galloping around the green, riding his putter like a stallion after a made putt, and autographing the eighty-year-old woman's chest just like he did the twenty-year-old woman's. For Tommy Boy fun is dancing and partying, hanging out with friends. He and his dad are tearing it up, dancing together, when his dad's fatal heart attack thrusts Tommy into the adult world. For Ty Webb fun is living the laid back life of the ultra cool, punctuated by the occasional dalliance. How can you help but smile when Ty bursts out singing, "I was born to love you. I was born to lick your face"? What female could resist such charm?

Not only are these characters genuine and fun loving, but they also *accept challenges*. Happy has to overcome not only his lack of experience, but also the death of a friend and mentor, the barbs of a rival, getting run over by a VW Bug on the course, and having to complete a trick shot over and through a downed media platform for the win. That sounds like a pretty average day for some of us, doesn't it? Happy's biggest challenge is his prodigious temper, though. Happy's temper gets him pummeled by celebrity golfer Bob Barker and leads him to threaten his nemesis Shooter with a broken beer bottle. It nearly gets him thrown off the tour. Happy has to learn how to calm down and "go to his happy place." I'm guessing few people's happy places are quite as risqué as Happy's, but there's nothing wrong with a little positive visualization. Tommy Boy certainly has challenges to overcome, too, and the stakes are high. If he fails, the brake empire his father built will be lost. Getting out from under his father's shadow while being true to his legacy is a challenge. When he starts, he's like the *Animal House* character that is told, "Fat, drunk, and stupid is no way to go through life, son." Tommy doesn't give up, he has faith, and in true movie fashion the good guy wins in the end. Ty Webb's challenges aren't as dramatic although he's happy taking a bet and comfortable being the anti-hero. To be honest, I think he made it into this group because this week is the British Open, I was watching *Happy Gilmore*, and I envy people who can actually golf. Ty is fearless, whether it's standing up to influential establishment figure Judge Smails or seducing Lacey Underall, the judge's niece. Ty epitomizes grace under pressure.

All of these guys are really just *finding their way* through life. While our lives aren't episodic hilarity like theirs for most of us, we have to find what works for us, too. Happy Gilmore is impulsive, of course, following the one-eyed gator who killed his mentor Chubs right into to the water to retrieve his ball from its mouth. He matures to possess a modicum of control, however. He learns not to chuck his clubs, and he learns how to focus. He understands the importance of practicing. He understands that sometimes you actually have to play by the rules. As for Tommy Boy, forget for a minute that he dresses up like a suicide bomber using road flares and that his company is saved by a series of miraculously improbable events. Instead, look at his power of persuasion and ability to read people. When he declares he is "on the side of the American working man," people believe him. In the end he finds his own voice and assumes the mantle of leadership, which we should all aspire to do. Ty Webb is finding his way like a movie version of the real life Zen master, Phil Jackson. Coach Jackson exuded calm as he won championships for the Bulls and Lakers, and

Ty Webb has that preternatural centeredness, too. "Be the ball," he advises young Danny Noonan, and he shows how in one of the great movie scenes, knocking in putts from all angles and directions while barefoot and blindfolded. Antagonist Judge Smails is obsessed with comparisons and judging himself (ironically enough) by others. Upon hearing Webb doesn't score his rounds, Smails asks him how he measures himself with other golfers. Webb's answer is classic: "By height." Webb embodies the farcical, like Oscar Wilde's great play *The Importance of Being Earnest*. Wilde loves to poke fun at what society takes too seriously, sharing gems like, "In matters of grave importance, style, not sincerity is the vital thing," and "I hate people who are not serious about meals. It is so shallow of them." I think Wilde would have approved of Webb's character.

I hope I haven't wasted your time today. I realize that if you haven't seen *Happy Gilmore, Tommy Boy,* and *Caddyshack*, you might be scratching your head. All I can say is, "Watch more cable." I toyed with using *Joe Dirt, Stripes, Billy Madison, Fletch, Vacation,* and *Step Brothers*. See, it could have been worse. Surely you can't argue with my main points: **be yourself, have fun, accept challenges, and find your way.** Take a minute and think of your own fictional characters or real people who reinforce these things for you. You won't be sorry!

1. Be yourself

• =

• =

2. Have fun

• =

• =

3. Face challenges

• =

• =

4. Find your way

• =

• =

Day 23:

Play

I am like a ten-year-old child with an old soul. That is an odd statement perhaps, but it is the closest I can come at this moment to capturing my personality. I take my responsibilities very seriously, but I don't take myself too seriously. I can't really take credit for this distinction since I used to have the following Peter Ustinov quote as my email signature: "It is our responsibilities, not ourselves, that we should take seriously." For me this is a good reminder to lighten up and remember it's not about us! One of my non-negotiables is that I am going to enjoy my work. That doesn't mean I don't know when to be serious or that I don't understand the enormous responsibility I have as a school administrator. More than likely my wife bears the brunt of my child-like nature, but she has stuck with me for 24 years and counting. She has accepted the responsibility of the occasional reminder: "Art, they don't know your sense of humor," when I might be exposing a stranger or acquaintance to too much too soon.

I have to make the point, though, that a lot of people a lot smarter than I am have stressed the importance of play. Plato (part of the triumvirate of great ancient Greek philosophers along with Socrates and Aristotle) said, "You can discover more about a person in an hour of play than in a year of conversation." This is very true. How do people act when they have let their guard down? What are they like when they aren't necessarily "on their best behavior"? Prospective employers are very intentional about getting this information sometimes, arranging for candidates to be put in social situations that are far less formal than an interview. I'm sure a lot of jobs have been won or lost in these situations. Today's job seekers are urged to consider their digital footprint, or web presence. This can be a selling point or a detriment, depending on one's online activity. Forbes Staff Writer Jacquelyn Smith notes that CareerBuilder. com found that 37% of employers use social networks to screen potential job candidates (www.forbes.com/sites/jacquelingsmith/2013/04/16/how-social-media-can-help-or-hurt-your-job-search/). I suspect that percentage will only rise in our hyper-connected world. My advice to new teachers this morning was to carefully think about their online presence. I went further, saying that the more exactly one's personal and public personas match, the better. In my book, it's about being genuine and transparent. I am who I am, and here it is. A person has to be secure to take that approach. I haven't always been that way; and if I were making bad decisions in my personal life, I couldn't be an open book in my professional life.

Another great writer and thinker, American Transcendentalist Ralph Waldo Emerson, weighed in on this topic of play. Emerson wrote, "It is a happy talent to know how to play." I love this simple quote. Have you ever thought of knowing how to play as a talent? Think of it the other way for a moment. Have you known people who seem to have no sense of humor or capacity for fun? Have you encountered people who seem to have no joy in living? I'm sure we all have. A sense of playfulness can be developed, like any other talent. It is not a natural thing for everyone. Attitudes are contagious, though, and it is easier to smile and enjoy oneself if that is the culture of one's job and home. If it isn't that way, maybe you can lead the change. Smile. Play. It's good for you!

Heraclitus, another Greek philosopher predating Plato, made a statement that really makes me think: "Time is a game played beautifully by children." Isn't it fun to watch a child at play, especially if it is simple, unscripted play without an electronic or parental interference? Kids can be in their own little world, engrossed in and captivated by the moment. This is play at its essence. Do you suppose we can incorporate a little bit of that child-like wonder into our adult lives? Can time be a game beautifully played by us? It's a topic at least worth thinking about. It's an attitude Henry David Thoreau captured when he wrote in *Walden*, "Time is but the stream I go a' fishing in."

Author Roald Dahl understood that this isn't an either/or proposition. We're not making a choice to either be a responsible adult or enjoy life (Jim Collins discusses the "tyranny of *or*" in his great book *Built to Last*. I recommend that book, a study of enduringly excellent companies). Dahl states very simply, "Life is more fun if you play games."

I know I'm on board with that. He also writes, "A little nonsense now and then, is cherished by the wisest men." (I just had a mental image of John Candy's character in *Stripes* saying, "Lighten up, Francis," to the anti-social soldier who said, "You call me Francis, I'll kill ya'.") A sense of fun, a little play, in our lives is important; and it seems like the importance increases in proportion to the seriousness or weightiness of a person's work. Maybe that's why some Presidents seem to be perpetually on vacation or on the golf course; they're just trying to maintain some life balance (I can't decide if I really mean that or if I'm saying it tongue-in-cheek).

Alan Watts, *The Way of Zen* author, offers an interesting thought that captures what I am trying to say about work and play pretty well: "This is the real secret of life—to be completely engaged with what you are doing in the here and now. And instead of calling it work, realize it is play." Life is short, sometimes tragically so. We do get opportunities to get our priorities straight and second chances to learn to enjoy life more sometimes. Sometimes we miss those opportunities or never get a second chance, though. I want to encourage you today to be <u>intentional</u> about enjoying what you are doing. Have a little fun. Inject some humor into your daily grind. <u>Play!</u>

Things I enjoy most about my work:
1.

2.

3.

Ways I can do more of the things I enjoy:

1.

2.

3.

Day 24:

Lost

I have heard my share of mechanized female voices saying, "If possible, make a U-turn," and "Recalculating," especially while we crisscrossed the Midwest in pursuit of the next gym one of our sons would be playing in. Rarely, if ever, were we truly lost even if we missed a turn or exit, though. We were never panicked, disoriented, or oblivious to land-marks (except for a couple of times I shouldn't have been driving in blizzard conditions).

All of these things—panic, disorientation, and oblivion—were present when I got lost in Rock Run as a boy. I was probably eight years old, maybe nine, and Rock Run was a wilderness paradise just five blocks or so from my house. Trails ran through dense foliage, and the explorer could venture down to a lively creek or up a rocky hillside. If one crossed under the Rocksylvania Street Bridge, walking was pretty much impossible, but the limestone cliffs beckoned an adventurous youngster. Rock Run is where I went one morning when I was "running away" on my bike, and I still remember the rabbits hopping across the path in front of me in the morning's dewy grass.

The day I got lost, it was much later, probably nearly dusk when I started exploring. I had crossed the ravine from west to east and was tramping along the hillside across the creek. The hillsides had been dumping grounds in the past, with the houses and businesses that ringed the top of Rock Run contributing their trash and treasures. I was "picking" before Mike and Frank even thought of it, bringing home old bottles and other treasures. I lost track of time this night and began to panic as it got dark. I became disoriented and really had no idea which direction I was going. I felt like I was in the bottom of a big, smooth-sided bowl, scrambling to get out. I couldn't see any landmarks even though the hospital and Merle's East Side Lounge weren't so far away. I was in a frenzy, scrambling on hands and knees, trying to get to the top of the hillside. I was LOST.

I finally emerged in a residential area, where most of the houses appeared tiny and dark. It was probably 9:00 P.M., late enough that my parents would be worried. A porch light down the street beckoned me, and a nice old lady pitied the scared, filthy boy with the tear-stained face. A taxi was whisking me home in minutes. I really can't remember the details. I don't know who paid for the cab or how my parents reacted. All I remember is the panic of being lost and the relief of being found.

I felt a momentary panic a couple of nights ago as I took off on my first hot air balloon ride. I definitely wasn't lost, though. In fact, once we got up in the air, I felt like I knew more and could see more than the people on the ground from my superior view and perspective.

Maybe that's how Louie Zamperini and the other World War II pilots felt, but it sounds like the peril they were in kept them from enjoying the view. I am thankful I never had to experience anything like being shot down, lost at sea, and finally delivered to land only to be tortured in Japanese POW camps. If you want to read a riveting account of human endurance, read Laura Hillenbrand's *Unbroken: A World War II Story of Survival, Resilience, and Redemption*. It is one of life's greatest ironies that sometimes people find themselves and realize what they are truly capable of when they are apparently hopelessly lost.

What really saddens me are the legions of people who are panicked, disoriented, and oblivious—truly lost—today without even knowing it. I have observed a lot of living in panic, bouncing from one crisis to another. I am not heartless; I know life throws people curves and people have to battle through tough times. People with direction persevere and make it through challenges, not always unscathed and not without help, but they aren't lost. Being lost brings panic. Life's lost souls are often disoriented, too. Many times they are in the grip of an addiction, surviving in a haze but not really living. Sometimes people seem to aimlessly wander through life because they don't have any landmarks—goals or guidance, for example.

I have probably been all of these people at one time. I will never be lost again, though. I know exactly where I am and where I'm going. I don't say that out of arrogance. I know I am a sinner and far from perfect. Through God's grace and the gift of His Son and the Spirit, I am much better than I was on my own. Because of my family, my life is worth much more than it would be without them. Because of meaningful work, it is much easier to find purpose in each day. These things keep me oriented; they are my landmarks. Faith, family, and work are the things I continually refer to as my Big Rocks, my reason for living. These things ensure that I will stay on the right path and not stray down dark alleys or lose my way. These are the things that help me enjoy this life and its challenges without panic or fear. Knowing my ultimate destination and having an iron clad promise that I will get there if I accept my guide is a comfort, too.

There is a simple reassurance given in Luke 19:10: "For the Son of Man came to seek and to save what was lost" (NIV). Jesus tells the recently saved Zaccheus this when he goes to the tax collector's house to eat. Louis Zamperini felt the truth of this. After the war he was haunted by what he had been through and descended into alcoholism and hopelessness. The great evangelist Billy Graham opened the door for the Spirit to convict Zamperini and remind him of a promise he had made in desperation on a life raft: "If you will save me, I will serve you forever" (*Unbroken*, 375). That's it in a nutshell: being saved is the opposite of being lost. We are all one or the other even though people resist that simple message today.

I hope that you aren't feeling lost today; but if you are, call out to God. He promised He would send the Spirit as a Comforter if you just ask. If you need that comfort, try this prayer as a starter:

Dear God,

I'm feeling lost, and I need Your comfort. Send Your Spirit to calm my soul. Help me feel Your presence and know that everything will be all right. Reassure me that You are in control and have a plan and a purpose for me. Strengthen me so that I am not a captive to doubt and sin. Help me to feel Your love and presence.

Amen

Day 25:

PR

What do you think of when you hear the two-letter acronym *PR?* Personal record? Public relations? I think my days of chasing personal records are over unless we are talking about my ever-burgeoning weight. Since I am currently engaged in a "getting to know you" blitzkrieg at my new job, I guess I will ruminate on public relations a little bit today.

Whether or not you consistently interact with the public in your career, I know you have experienced positive and negative PR. I am willing to bet there is a fast food chain or grocery store chain you feel more positively or more negatively toward based on your experience with a clerk at the register. If you routinely have positive experiences at that place, chances are the chain understands PR and knows that its hourly employees, or minimum wage type workers, are the face of the organization. My assumption is that those positive PR chains pay attention to organizational culture.

Smart leaders know what image their organization projects to the public, and they understand that morale and job satisfaction "in the trenches" impact PR in many cases.

I write as an authority here because I have watched "Undercover Boss" a few times and enjoy the show's premise. The boss gets out in the field and sees things through the eyes of the company's hourly employees. He/she gains an appreciation for the workers' contributions and points-of-view and observes first-hand how the employees interact with the public. It's generally a feel-good, appreciate-the-little-guy kind of show. Another type of show I watch sometimes is the restaurant undercover sting show, like "Restaurant Stakeout" and "Mystery Diners." "Bar Rescue" is good, too. In these shows a concerned owner who is hemorrhaging money invites an outside expert in to view hidden camera footage and send undercover operatives in. Generally the business is plagued by poor customer service, lack of training, indifference, conspicuous lack of leadership, and even theft. The tone of the show is usually different than "Undercover Boss," but both types of shows highlight the importance of the "boss" knowing what is going on in the organization and not being out of touch. In education parlance this is called situational awareness, one of MCREL's *21 Leadership Responsibilities* discussed in Balanced Leadership training.

It is impossible, or at the very least impractical and unhealthy, for an organization's leader to be on top of or in control of every minute detail of the organization. However, he/she should help drive culture and should be aware of what is going on. People throughout the organization need to know the leader cares about what is happening, and they need to know their work is important and appreciated. It is a fundamental truth that everyone, the boss included, does better work when there is accountability and support. People need to have their best traits and efforts engaged and reinforced, or there will be backsliding and indifference.

I am offering a broad definition of public relations here, and I fully appreciate that not everyone is comfortable with or skilled in PR pursuits. I want to bring the conversation down to a level that applies to everyone, though. I want us to think about what we communicate in our relationships with others. Consider the following examples:

Listening:

Good PR: being fully present, making eye contact, positive non-verbal cues

Bad PR: being distracted, checking cell phone, interrupting

Which one says, "You are worth listening to, and you have my attention"?

Returning Calls/Emails:

Good PR: immediate response, access, awareness of tone in emails and voice mails

Bad PR: delayed response or ignoring altogether, being brusque or unfriendly

Which one says, "I want to work with you, and I appreciate your input"?

Acknowledging Effort:

Good PR: authentic acknowledgement, both personal and public; thanks for work well done

Bad PR: assuming people know they are appreciated, thinking there is not need to affirm work being done well as expected

Which environment would you rather work in, thankful or thankless?

Being Polite:

Good PR: saying please and thank you, opening a door for others, extending dignity to all

Bad PR: not bothering with niceties, especially to a subordinate

Should it make any difference what a person's position is? Isn't every person entitled to the same level of human dignity?

Being Thankful, not Entitled:

Good PR: servant leadership, living at the foot of the cross

Bad PR: demanding your due, insisting on your own parking space

What kind of boss would you enjoy more?

Seeing the Good in People:

Good PR: meeting people where they are, building on strengths, giving the benefit of the doubt

Bad PR: focusing on the negative, running people down, assuming the worst

Which one of these approaches makes the other actions easier? If you see the good in someone, is it easier to listen, be accessible, compliment them, be polite, and be thankful?

This is nothing new. You have heard someone say, "It's all about relationships." Those aren't just words. John Maxwell speaks and writes about "adding value"; that should be our goal for any organization we are a part of. Rick Warren wrote, "The greatest gift you can give somebody is your attention because your attention is your time, and your time is your life. You're never going to get it back, and that's why it is so precious when you give it." Resist the temptation to say, "I don't have the time of day for that person." Make time. Think about PR. Really PR means "personal relationships" as much as it means "public relations." Give your best to the world and all the people in it. You will not be disappointed! People will respond to that, and you will realize that there are a lot of great people out there. You will benefit from positive relationships, and, most importantly, you will become a better person.

Have a great day!

Day 26:

Character

I am a man of character, and I deserve very little credit for this. The people, circumstances, and events of my life have helped develop character within me. In many cases positive experiences and admirable people have reinforced and encouraged strong character. At other times my character has been formed or tested in response to grief, disappointment, and despicable people. Henry Ford had it exactly right when he said, "Life is a series of experiences, each one of which makes us bigger, even though sometimes it is hard to realize this. For the world was built to develop character, and we must learn that the setbacks and grieves which we endure help us in our marching onward" (www.brainyquote.com).

I understand Ford focuses on the character building of hardships and setbacks. How we respond to the inevitable setbacks of life predicts our future; I am convinced of this. I believe in the self-fulfilling prophecy. People who can handle disappointment without becoming bitter and negative are simply more optimistic and hopeful, which makes them much more attractive to others. I once had a big professional disappointment, which I accepted stoically and learned from. Very shortly afterward, within a few weeks, I had an opportunity to advance professionally. I was on a new track that delivered two more tremendous opportunities that I could not have conceived of five years earlier. I am convinced that these opportunities came because I was at peace with the situation, determined to stay positive, and trusted that God would give me opportunities to use gifts He has given me to serve others.

Besides the loss of loved ones, I have not had severe trials and suffering in my life. Everyone has to work through grief when loved ones die, and I claim no special character for doing that. My mother, whom I have written about before, certainly displayed her character in the face of trial and suffering, though. My mom understood suffering and endurance from a young age. Burned badly at age four, she had skin grafts over 80% of her body. She worked hard and did without her whole life. Just as she and my father were preparing to enjoy retirement, he was killed and she was paralyzed in a car accident. Through it all (and the subsequent bouts of cancer that eventually killed her) my mother was amazingly positive and faithful. She showed everyone who knew her what true character and courage are. She was a fine example of what Helen Keller, another great woman of character, described: "Character cannot be developed in ease and quiet. Only through experience of trial and suffering can the soul be strengthened, ambition inspired, and success achieved" (www.brainyquote.com).

Character is not merely a result of suffering, though. I began this entry writing, "I am a man of character." In large part this is true because over 24 years ago I married a wonderful woman, and she makes me better than I am on my own. "A noble wife is her husband's crown," Proverbs states, and that is exactly how I feel (Proverbs 12:4, NIV). We raised two incredible sons, and the responsibility I felt to be a good role model for them contributed to character development in me. I have known many clergy, educators, and coaches who have been positive forces in my life. They gave me opportunities to grow, and I saw them demonstrate great humility and character when they could have been impressed with themselves instead.

I have had meaningful work to do in which strong character is very important. As a teacher, coach, school administrator, and church leader I have been constantly aware that I am a public figure and people are watching me. I strive to make my public self and my private self the same person. I want to be genuine. I want to demonstrate character.

We all know that people sometimes make assumptions about people that aren't true. We have all done this. I believe what Henry David Thoreau once wrote: "Public opinion is a weak tyrant compared with our own private opinion" (*Walden*). I don't dismiss the power of reputation, though, especially when it can reflect upon my faith, my family, and my work (my Big Rocks). Abe Lincoln once said, "Character is like a tree and reputation like a shadow. The shadow is what we think of it; the tree is the real thing" (www.brainyquote.com). I agree. My personal character is the real thing, just as yours is. However, the shadow gives us a pretty darned good idea of what the tree is like sometimes. How do you want to be known and remembered? Your reputation is a reflection of your character.

I hope you can make the statement, "I am a person of character." If you can't, then your focus should be, "To become a person of character, I must..." Take a minute right now and consider your attitudes and actions that display your positive character.

Signs of my character:

(at work)   1.

                    2.

                    3.

(at home)   1.

                    2.

                    3.

(at church)   1.

                    2.

                    3.

(in the community) 1.

                    2.

                    3.

(in relationships) 1.

                    2.

                    3.

Your character is more valuable than any material thing you own! What is the state of your character?

Day 27:

Decisions

Recently I heard Dan Heath, co-author of *Made to Stick*, *Switch*, and *Decisive*, speak at the School Administrators of Iowa conference. The general topic was how to make better decisions, and an audience of school administrators would seem to be a fitting audience for this topic (Insert snide comment here). I often tell administrators with whom I work that they are hired to make decisions. People expect that of well-compensated employees, and every administrator has heard, "That's why you make the big bucks." I probably should emphasize making good decisions, not just decisions. Heath discussed four villains that lead to bad decisions, and all of us—not just school administrators—would do well to avoid them. Let me list them here, and then I will delve into each one individually:

1. Narrow Framing

2. Confirmation Bias

3. Short-term Emotion

4. Overconfidence

I'm pretty sure that you will think of annoying know-it-alls or opinionated people you know as we explore these four villains of bad decisions, but it is my sincere hope that we are self-aware and reflect on our own decision-making practices, too!

Narrow Framing, as it relates to decisions, really refers to not allowing ourselves options. Heath calls these "whether or not decisions" and compares these to how teenagers habitually think. Business guru Jim Collins refers to this mindset as the "tyranny of the 'or'." The late Stephen Covey urged people to engage in "third alternative" thinking. Many times there is another option or a middle ground if we will just let ourselves see it.

For example, I don't get enough exercise, and some nights I don't feel like getting any. I just want to sit in my chair and read or watch TV. My wife, however, would always be up for a four-mile walk (which I refer to as a forced march). It doesn't have to be a brisk four-mile walk or nothing. How about a four-mile bike ride or a three-mile walk? I'm tired, perhaps, but I bet I could do that. To avoid narrow framing, widen your options and open yourself to a new world of possibilities. I would add one caveat: there are limited areas where one clear choice exists, and there really aren't options. Jesus says, "You're with me, or you're against me." A spouse expects faithfulness 24/7. You get the idea.

Confirmation bias is sneaky and self-serving, and we all fall prey to it. If you had two books of data in front of you, *Data That Supports My Opinion* and *Data That Contradicts My Opinion*, which one would be more appealing to you to look at? We all see the world through the lens of our values and beliefs, and we all like to think we're right. We read and listen to information that supports what we believe, and we hang out with like-minded people. The feedback we get naturally supports what we believe, and we take this as confirmation that we are right. Maybe we are most of the time, but we can learn a lot from our critics. I personally believe we should seek data or information from opposing sources, if for no other reason, to understand the opposition. Feedback is critical. Cognitive dissonance promotes reflection and growth. Put on your big boy (or big girl) panties and learn to consciously combat confirmation bias. Listen to divergent opinions. If you are right, you will strengthen your stance. If not, hopefully you're open to growth and change.

There probably is no more striking example of this process than Saul of Tarsus, who became the Apostle Paul. Saul was dedicated to stamping out Christianity. He was a committed persecutor of Christians and was a very devoted person to his own religion. He certainly had a confirmation bias and was convinced he was doing God's work *until* he had his Damascus road experience, when Jesus asked from the blinding light, "Saul, Saul, why are you persecuting Me?" (Acts 9:4, NIV) Can you imagine how different Christianity might be today if Saul had not become Paul, nurturing the early church and spreading the Gospel to the Gentiles? We might never get this dramatic a wake up call, but I hope we are open to things outside of our worldview, or we will never grow, and our decision-making will suffer.

Short-term emotion, hopefully, loses a little bit of its grip on us as we mature. I have seen a lot of stupid decisions made by adults in the "heat of the moment," though. For behavior disordered students impulsivity is a huge problem. These children's emotions of the moment rule their behavior. They have no filters or no ways to put the brakes on. Don't get smug; it's not just the kids. Have you ever suffered buyer's remorse? As I wrote this, I was sitting in the Varied Industries Building at the Iowa State Fair. All kinds of hot tub, cutlery, mattress, sunroom, and gutter cover salespeople would have <u>loved</u> me to be impulsive! I have the credit card debt to prove I've done it before, but I'm learning to master short-term emotion. We should not be guided solely by our emotions in making decisions. You know people who are. Their bad day is always everyone else's bad day! Get some distance. Take a breath. Count to ten. Have accountability partners who will help you put your short-term emotion aside.

The last trap was *overconfidence*. I golf every now and then so that I stay humble and remember how wrong and inadequate I can be. I'm also married with children, so my family is helpful in this arena. I am a huge believer in confidence, but beware of overconfidence. Heath says, "Prepare to be wrong." Collins writes, "Practice productive paranoia." If you are overconfident and can't conceive of being wrong or disappointed, look out! The ancient Greeks called it *hubris*. The Bible warns, "Pride goeth before destruction, and an haughty spirit before a fall" (Proverbs 16:18 KJV).

We have to be ready to adapt, learn, and move on when we are wrong. (I just had a flashback to a "Happy Days" episode, when the Fonz can't make himself say he was wrong.) Seriously, how much learning takes place when you are right? Reinforcement, yes. Learning, I'm not sure. We should make decisions with as much confidence as possible and as much certainty as possible, but the more complex the situation or decision, the more likely we will be at least partially wrong. In some cases the "right" decision for one is the "wrong" decision for another, which illustrates an administrative truism: you are never going to please everybody. We can't let that crush us when we are wrong or partially wrong. Acknowledge the bad decision or the difficult situation. Try to learn from it. Be determined not to replicate it if possible.

Overconfident people usually don't respond well to adversity. They fall apart when their bubble of invincibility is burst or their worldview is turned upside down. Over-confident people have situations go from bad to worse very quickly. I value resilience, toughness, and being able to roll with the punches about as much as anything. I learned that from my mom, among others. Biblically, the Pharisees were overconfident people, and Jesus targeted their pompous hypocrisy continuously. It was the rare Pharisee who saw the truth of what Jesus had to say.

I really believe avoiding these four traps will help you tremendously in your decision-making, and if I've piqued your interest, I suggest you buy Dan Heath's book. Have a great day!

Day 28:

Possibilities

When I began teaching in the fall of 1988 in Fairfax, MO, I had no idea what the future held. In fact, I began my teaching career intending to quit and go to law school if I didn't like it. I worked hard—teaching, coaching, and driving the bus to activities—and I netted $1,133.00 a month. (Let me offer an amusing side note: I got my bus license by driving my 1979 Monte Carlo for an examiner. I was licensed before I had ever driven a bus. Go figure.) I gained valuable experience and met some wonderful people in Fairfax during my first two years as an educator, but I was young and selfish and focused mostly on myself. I had no idea what I might experience or accomplish, but our God is a God of possibilities.

Twenty-six years later, I know without question that my wife Cindy came to me as a gift from God during that time, and He blessed us with two sons, too. As a young family man, my priorities began to guide my actions, and a world of possibilities opened up to me. After we moved back to Iowa, Cindy and I coached together for eleven years while our sons grew up, and we became a "basketball family." I look back on those years fondly and contrast my experience with that of some other coaches, who made it all about their career and destroyed their marriages.

Everyone has possibilities in life. In order to take advantage of them, people have to do their part, though. They need to do the work to position themselves for success, and they need to be open to new things. Each of these actions is of critical importance. Let me tackle them in order.

For me, positioning myself for success really just meant working hard and trying to become better. In my case that was earning an M.A. in English literature, later graduate work in education leadership, and becoming a licensed minister. At the same time I was working hard professionally and trying to grow, and my family was blessed to find a caring church family to grow in. Working at one's spiritual life is even more important than one's professional life. If one's spiritual house is in order, then one is positioned for success in one's personal life and professional life. I am not suggesting that a personal relationship with Christ and a life leading to eternal salvation are merely means to material, or worldly, success. Prosperity preachers walk this line sometimes. What I am saying is that the more attuned we become to God's Will for our lives, the more blessed we will be. God will open doors we never imagined. As the Bible promises, "Seek ye first the kingdom of God, and His righteousness; and all these things shall be added unto you" (Matthew 6:33 KJV). Leading a spiritual life is work, though. That's why prayer, worship, and Bible study are called *spiritual disciplines*. These disciplines become labors of love for the believer, however.

We can't work our way to salvation, and it is possible to toil in vain. That's why being open to possibility is as important as positioning ourselves for success. As I look back on what has been a very satisfying and productive career in education, I find that many of the great opportunities and times of growth have found me, and I just needed to say, "Yes." In fact, sometimes I had other plans of my own. I have found over and over that God's plans are better than our plans.

For example, I never intended to become a school administrator, I thought ministry might be a retirement job, and I doubted I would ever write a book. God had other plans, and he used people and events in my life to bring me along. In the mid-1990s my principal (a good friend who recently retired from the superintendency and now pastors a church) came to my classroom and asked me if I would consider serving as activities director. If I agreed, I would still be teaching six periods of English a day and coaching, but I would gain valuable experience and a $6,000 stipend. I was open to the possibility and worked hard at it, and being A.D. was my bridge to education leadership classes and later administrative positions. A few years later my pastor started suggesting that I enter the Licensed Minister Education Program for the Christian Church of the Upper Midwest. I resisted for a while because my plan was to possibly minister in retirement, which was far off. By the mid 2000s I was doing pulpit fill, which led to my enrolling in the program. This past summer I wrapped up a stint of over two years of service as a bi-vocational pastor. It was an honor and a blessing to pastor a church of great people who needed leadership during a time of transition. If I had stuck to my plan, I would never have gotten to serve this way.

So often, being open to possibilities just means saying, "Yes," or, more realistically, "All right, I suppose I'll give it a try," when opportunity knocks. Sometimes people see potential in us before we recognize it ourselves. I was never the greatest, most accomplished basketball coach, but I met tremendous people, got to coach all-stars, worked great camps, served on boards and in leadership positions, and went on some truly memorable trips: all because I said, "Yes," and then worked hard to do my best. Many times my wife or sons were partners in these ventures. I can say without reservation that these coaching experiences were as valuable as anything else in preparing me for success as a school administrator.

Administratively I have been blessed because of saying yes to possibilities, too. I have had opportunities to serve on boards and fill leadership roles. I have had the opportunity to be an educational leader for other administrators. I have helped others work hard to be their best and say yes to opportunities. I say this with no personal pride. Just the opposite—almost anyone who works hard to position himself/herself for success and then says yes to opportunities can achieve good things.

Everyone has heard, "Success breeds success." That's true in our lives. Our lives are a body of work. Success gives us the confidence to take risks and try new things, which leads to more success. People are drawn to others who display confidence and have a track record of success, and they offer up more possibilities.

There are at least two dangers we face once we have enjoyed success: complacency and arrogance. Complacency very quickly becomes stagnation or laziness. Once we become self-satisfied, it seems less important to strive to become better. We quit growing. Soon our spiritual lives are flabby, we're taking our family for granted, or we're "phoning it in" at work. Beware of complacency! Remember, working to position ourselves for future possibilities was what brought opportunity to our door. Arrogance is a trap, too. Before we know it, arrogance can lead us to trust only in ourselves. We can become so confident that we don't honor the source of our abilities and strength, God. The efforts of arrogant people are only about their comfort, not about working hard and serving others.

I am saddened when I think about the many people in the world who see no hope, no possibilities in life. I really believe that if they could focus on working hard to position themselves for future possibilities and would be prepared to say yes when opportunities arose, hope would make an appearance in their lives. For those people suffering hardships that make finding hope difficult, we should be in prayer and should extend Christian charity when we can. We should also share our stories of success, giving credit where it's due. I pray that each one of us will work hard to make the most of opportunities given to us and will remain open to new possibilities!

Day 29:
The Mantle of Leadership

In Shakespeare's *Henry IV* the king is sleepless one night, musing about his subjects slumbering and ending his soliloquy saying, "Uneasy lies the head that wears a crown" (Part 2, Act 3, Scene 1). The king was obviously feeling the weight of leadership. Often this idea is expressed, "Heavy is the head that wears the crown." I have not done a study, but the actual physical weight of ancient crowns might have contributed to this expression. Somewhere in my memory banks I remember hearing about a king whose crown was so heavy that two people had to help hold his head up. Certainly the famous bejeweled crowns of gold would have some heft to them. The heaviest crown of all, though, had to be the crown of thorns mockingly thrust upon the head of Christ because it came with the weight of all of the sins of the world.

I am going to generalize just a bit from the crown of the monarchy to the mantle of leadership. Many more people will be leaders than royalty, but there are a lot of people who are not comfortable with the mantle of leadership. Why is that? Let's take a few minutes to consider why Henry IV was having a sleepless night, what it was that immortalized Jesus as King of Kings, and how we can become more comfortable in the role of leader.

Leaders accept responsibility.

It takes courage to step up and say, "I'll do that." Sometimes the challenge is momentous, and the acceptance sounds more like, "I'll do my best." Leaders become more comfortable than the average person with putting their name on the line and taking a risk, often very publicly. Accepting responsibility in its purest form is being willing to adopt a "the buck stops here" mentality (possibly not adopted by any U.S. President since Harry S. Truman). The only dangers I see in accepting responsibility are wanting to take credit when things go well and deflect blame when they don't. Neither of those things is in the true spirit of responsibility. Accepting responsibility is <u>tough</u>. Even Jesus prayed to God, seeking another way than the cross (Mark 14:36, Luke 22:42). In the end He did it, though. Accepting responsibility means doing what needs to be done when it isn't easy.

Leaders sacrifice.

The heart of sacrifice is putting others first. Children should learn about leadership from their parents first, as they see their parents sacrifice for them. I know this doesn't always happen. It can be difficult to understand the sacrifices leaders make if one hasn't been in a leadership position, just as it can be difficult to understand what parenting is like before one has done it. People more readily see the benefits of leadership, which often include increased compensation and authority. They don't always see the costs of leadership: the leader's constant "on call" status, the time away from family or personal pursuits, the toll of making weighty decisions, etc. I know I have encountered aspiring administrators whom I suspect are seeing the benefits and not the costs. We get a little glimpse of this phenomenon as we look at the before and after pictures of U.S. Presidents before their term(s) in office and afterwards. There is a cost to leadership. For Jesus Christ the cost was extreme physical agony leading to death. An even greater cost was the spiritual agony of separation from God the Father as Jesus became the scapegoat for our sins. Jesus was the best leader of all time, and He was honest with His followers (as the best leaders are): "Whoever wants to be my disciple must deny themselves and take up their cross and follow me" (Matthew 16:24, NIV).

Leaders are symbols.

Jesus had an infallible understanding of who He was and why He was sent to earth (I do not mean to indicate by the past tense that He is not alive; He is). He understood that His leadership would leave a legacy that would speak through the ages. All leaders need to be comfortable with the idea of legacy and the symbolic nature of being a leader. Whether the leader is a teacher, coach, pastor, or CEO, the position is symbolic. If someone accepts that position and the accompanying title, it is analogous to putting on the mantle of leadership. In the age of social media, this is more important than ever to understand. A leader's words and actions are going to be closely scrutinized. Separating the personal and private lives becomes very difficult. I would contend that the best leaders do not have markedly different personal and private lives. They are who they are. They are genuine. They are not chameleons. There have been some notable political flameouts when aspiring leaders tried to be all things to all people. Nevertheless, genuine or not, our society likes to idealize leaders right up to the point when they have the opportunity to knock them down. My advice would be to understand the symbolic importance of leaders to people, be humble and genuine, and don't do stupid things that give people the opportunity to bring you down.

Leaders make decisions impacting others.

Another aspect of leadership is being willing to make decisions that affect other people. Of course, this leads right into the fact that leaders can't make everybody happy and shouldn't focus on that. Some people simply do not want to have to decide for others; to do so can be very uncomfortable. Leaders who wear the mantle of leadership comfortably and effectively try to involve others in decision-making, especially those affected by the decision. In situations where there are winners and losers, leaders have to try to help people understand the decision and maintain their dignity. Great leaders consistently have a positive impact on others. As John Quincy Adams wrote, great leaders inspire others to "dream more, learn more, do more, and become more."

Leaders handle complexity.

One thing any leader probably agrees to is that life is complicated. There is a complexity to leadership that some people just don't want. There are people who simply want well-defined parameters within which doing a good job is largely in their control. Leaders tend to want a challenge and are more comfortable with complexity and ambiguity. Because of the complex nature of leadership, it is critically important that leaders operate according to simple guiding principles. For example, "Be honest, work hard, and treat people right," would be guiding principles that would help any CEO navigate the rigors and complexities of running an organization. Life becomes much more manageable and enjoyable for all of us when we live our core beliefs.

I encourage all of us to have our eyes wide open about the demands of leadership and then step forward and say, "Bring it on," as we put that mantle on!

Day 30:

Legacy

In 2002, I was president of the Iowa Basketball Coaches' Association, and another executive board member and coach asked me, "What is your legacy going to be as president?" At the time I didn't even consider the question seriously. Doing so implied attaching too much significance to my service as president and me, I thought. In the last few days I have had things come up that made me think about legacy, and if that colleague asked me the same question today, I think I would answer it differently.

One of the things that made me think this way was catching a few minutes of the movie *Pay it Forward* last night. I watched *Lone Survivor* as well, which could have legacy implications, too, but let's focus on *Pay it Forward*. Of course, the expression and the idea of paying it forward is well engrained in our society now, and I happen to think it is a beautiful thing. I understand that thoughtful gestures happened long before someone expressed it this way, but I think it is a lasting gift, a legacy, that people are now so cognizant of paying it forward. I say that for two reasons: because of the awareness of one's own blessings and the determination to share them with others.

The other thing that made me think of legacy is that after a presentation I made to district employees at "District Day," during which I fondly remembered my Uncle Art, a former district employee, two different employees came up to me to let me know how kind and thoughtful Uncle Art had been to them. This is similar to the phenomenon I experience with former students of my father's kindly remembering him. That's a pretty cool legacy, one that I hope is repeated many times with people I have taught, coached, or served.

As I think about leaving a legacy, I know that my faith, my family (through both marriage and parenting), and my work are going to be the primary vehicles through which I leave a legacy. I can leave a legacy through my faith by setting a good Christian example and sharing the Good News. I have had the advantage of being a Sunday school teacher, elder, choir member, and pastor. I have been able to formally share God' glory in the classroom, from the pulpit, at weddings and funerals, and in the baptistery. I leave a legacy for my sons by being a supportive father but one who has been a parent first, then a friend. I like to think they have learned hard work and discipline, among other things, from me. I am richly blessed by their mother and them. I don't claim to be the dream husband, but I hope I have modeled what a strong marriage looks like along with my wife, too. In my work I have modeled professionalism and ethics. I have been willing to tackle challenges. One of my biggest legacies, I hope, is that people I work with know how much I appreciate them. I also have left a legacy of fun wherever I have been, I believe. The areas I have written about in this paragraph go right back to my Big Rocks, faith, family, and work. These are all areas I really want to have a lasting positive impact, which is what I think of when I hear *legacy*.

We don't always know or understand the impact we are having. Sometimes legacy unfolds over time after we are gone. We can be sure, though, that we are having a positive impact if we do as God desires. I have always liked this direction: "And what does the Lord require of you? To act justly and to love mercy and to walk humbly with your God" (Micah 6:8, NIV). I am positive that if we do these things, we will get the best confirmation ever of the legacy we have left when we go to meet our Maker: "Well done, good and faithful servant!" (Matthew 25:23, NIV).

Take a few minutes today and think about the legacy you are leaving. What are some signs that you are on the right track?

Have a blessed day!

Day 31:

Read!

I was musing last night about how different my life would be if I weren't a reader. Reading has brought me so much knowledge and joy through the years. It has challenged me, equipped me, and brought me escape. It has made me think, made me smile, and sometimes made me sleepy (Non-readers can relate to that last one!).

My earliest experiences with reading that I can remember were my mom reading to me as a small boy at bedtime. My mom was a farm girl herself, and I think she really enjoyed the Laura Ingalls Wilder tales that she read to me. *Little House on the Prairie* is the first book I remember.

Today most students are reading in kindergarten. I attended kindergarten half days and don't remember any reading instruction. I didn't go to pre-school either but lived in a literature rich home. I had some kind of foundation when I got to first grade because I took off reading with the SRA reading kits. By second grade I was going to the public library on the next block, reading all of the Cowboy Sam books. The next series I tackled was the Hardy Boys mystery series. I must have had a violent streak in fifth and sixth grade because I read every Mack Bolan, *The Executioner*, book and every *Destroyer* book I could get my hands on. As I got older, my tastes became more eclectic although I still like to find an author I enjoy and read everything he/she writes.

I have always read a lot. I vividly remember how incensed my eighth grade speech teacher was when I was reading while she talked. In high school sometimes I dragged through the school day after staying up reading into the wee hours of morning. In my early-married years I used to embarrass my wife by bringing a book to read to baseball and softball games. At the time I think I was A.D. and expected to be at all of the home baseball and softball games. As a basketball fan, I thought those summer sports dragged a little. That's my story, and I'm sticking to it!

I still read a lot today. It keeps me sharp and helps me grow. I use the public library quite a bit since I have had to sacrifice untold numbers of my books through various moves. Additional considerations are that my wife gets annoyed by books lying all over, and carrying boxes of books has not gotten easier as the years pass. The last two weeks I have read two mystery thrillers, a book on management theory, and a book about a U.S. President. I am conditioned to take notes on anything I think I can learn from or re-use. My wife once told me I don't know how to relax, and that's why I enjoy those books that are purely for enjoyment. I am able to just relax and read (and prove my wife wrong).

The most important daily reading I do is Bible reading. I am always working a "Read the Bible in a Year" plan; there are a number of those available. Bible reading is a spiritual discipline like prayer and worship, and having assigned Scripture each day is a more disciplined approach. As a Christian, I believe God's Word is the source of true wisdom. It's also the rare book that continues to deliver new insights on multiple readings. We are extremely privileged to have the Bible so readily available to us!

I also do quite a bit of electronic reading although I am old school and prefer a bound book to eBooks. I read blogs from the *Harvard Business Review*, which I access through LinkedIn. Twitter provides some good education articles and discussions. It's probably a stretch to consider Facebook serious reading most of the time, but it rounds out my trifecta of social media. There are many apps that can provide quick reads, too. I start each morning with a daily Bible verse on my smart phone; and I also get Fox News alerts, USA Today Pulse, and Flipboard. I will appreciate a good, old-fashioned newspaper as long as we can get them, too.

I can hardly imagine what it would be like not to be able to read. To me, that would be like being imprisoned in myself. The world is literally at our fingertips, and we can learn from the great thinkers and artists of yesteryear and today. We can assimilate the thoughts of the best and brightest into our own worldviews when it makes sense to. I find myself constantly referring to things I have read in interviews, speeches, and conversations. Reading is central to my being an effective leader; John Maxwell had it right when he said, "Not all readers are leaders, but all leaders are readers," in my humble opinion.

I am not going to be some kind of intellectual elite and look down on people who don't love to read. I have many shortcomings of my own. For example, I am the least mechanical man on the planet now that my dad has passed. I will make a final plea, though, (which seems pretty safe if you're already reading this book) that you reconnect with the joy, the utility, and the enlightenment of reading. Pick up that book you've wanted to read and haven't gotten around to. Go browse the public library without a plan. Kick back after work and read the paper. Read a book to your kid or grandkid. Volunteer to read to elementary students. Read the product manual for your new appliance (Kidding on that one! I get physically ill thinking about instruction manuals).

Start out by thinking about reading for a second.

Best book(s) I've ever read:

1.

2.

Book(s) I've been meaning to read:

1.

2.

Type(s) of reading I do:

1.

2.

Commitment to read that I will make right now:

Here's a link for a "Great Books" list of the classics: http://www.welltrainedmind.com/great-books/

Day 32:

Glory Days

I just crammed myself into a thirty-year-old shooting shirt and letter jacket to video an ALS ice bucket challenge (a cause which has generated over $70 million for ALS research in less than a month). A teammate on our great 1984 Iowa Falls Cadet Basketball Team nominated me, and I stuck with a theme since he was wearing a retro uniform. It was fun (and funny) because I am 70 pounds heavier and gray-haired now, and my arthritic knees have me decidedly earthbound. There were a lot of fun times back then, some accomplishments, good memories, and just a few regrets. As I write today, I have Bruce Springsteen, "the Boss's" song "Glory Days" running through my head.

There are people who are trapped in their memories of the past, and that's sad. You have met them. When they have a few too many beers, the volume goes up as they argue about some play in a game they were in 25 years ago.

Or maybe they're just a little too overbearing or expert in one of their kids' games even if they never played that sport themselves. They would like nothing more than to go back to those glory days.

The only reason I'd want to go back is to treat people better and make fewer dumb decisions. "Young and stupid" probably describes how I was at times. I'd like to have the physical ability and energy I had then with the accumulated wisdom and experience I have now. That's not the way it works, though, and with good reason. We have to have something to live for and look forward to, and we have to come to realize that it's not about us. If we have life all figured out at the height of our powers, we'd be insufferable!

I don't want to let this topic go by without mentioning the real Glory Days we have to look forward to, though! Wouldn't it make a lot more sense to look forward to glory days than to reminisce about them? The best is certainly yet to come: that's the premise all believers share and the idea behind the "Keep Your Fork" story (See Appendix J).

I believe God wants us to enjoy the here and now. It matters how we live our lives; otherwise God would not have sent the world the Law via Moses and the New Covenant in Christ. The purpose of a believer is to glorify God, and we do that by how we live our lives, faithfully and joyfully. We strive to make every day a "glory day" because we are walking in the light, and each day is a great blessing! As great as life is today, it is merely a shadow of what is to come. You've heard the expression, "He's a shadow of his former self." Well, I believe we're a shadow of our future self. There is no limit to what God can do with us.

I fondly remember my parents, family vacations, card games with friends, going to rummage sales and antique shops, delicious home-cooked meals, and so many other glorious memories from my childhood. I have a full complement of family memories with my wife and sons, too. I am so thankful for the opportunities and the time we've had together. I know, though, that all of those great times, those glory days, will pale in comparison to being in God's presence with my family. God promises no more tears and no more pain to my parents, and others, who have had their share of those things. He promises the glory of oneness with Him, no longer confined by our mortal bodies or sinful nature.

I love my life now. I am thankful for good memories. I look forward to those glory days of the future with God, though, and I hope you do, too!

Day 33:

Patience

(Disclaimer: I am a Cubs fan, for whom "maybe next year" and patient endurance are realities of life, and I am thinking the current crop of prospects might take the Cubs to the top someday.)

Proverbs 16:32 says, "Better a patient person than a warrior, one with self-control than one who takes a city" (NIV). Which one of those labels describes you better, a patient person or a warrior? Do you speed up and ride the bumper of the car ahead of you to prevent that annoying vehicle on your right from cutting in? Or do you patiently let off the gas and wave that driver who is in such a hurry in ahead of you? I can't even offer a response to that simple question. I am Dr. Jekyll and Mr. Hyde when it comes to patience, depending on my mood and the topic. I can be patient and understanding, or I can be looking for a fight.

I know my wife gets a little <u>impatient</u> with me because I always want a plan and a schedule. "When, exactly, are we going to eat and where?" is a frequent inquiry of mine. As a side note, I typically know what I'm going to order when I walk into a restaurant, and my wife is notorious for not being able to make up her mind. I joke that my life revolves around my next meal, but in life, if we are always impatiently focused on what's next, can we ever enjoy the present?

As I was writing this, I was thinking of the old adage, "Patience is a virtue." When I was looking for the author, I ran across this delightful variation: "Patience is a virtue, possess it if you can. Seldom found in woman, never found in man" (http://en.thinkexist.com/quotations/patience). That quote really puts a fine point on it.

My parents, especially my mom, had almost supernatural patience with my siblings and me. I'm positive I was not quite so patient with our sons. Speaking of supernatural patience, can you comprehend God's patience with us? How disappointing must we be as children? We make the same mistakes (commit the same sins) over and over again. We are selfish, willful, and disobedient, like petulant little children. We ignore His clear direction and take for granted His forgiveness. We fail to appreciate that He gave everything to redeem us and reunite us with Him: "For God so loved the world that He gave His only Son, that whoever believes in Him will not perish but have eternal life" (John 3:16, NIV). I am very thankful that we serve a loving God <u>and</u> a patient God!

One of the great Biblical examples of patience is Jacob, the man God renamed *Israel* and blessed greatly. Jacob loved Laban's daughter Rachel and agreed to tend Laban's flocks for seven years to win her hand. When the time came, he ended up with Rachel's Plain Jane ("weak-eyed") older sister Leah. Can you imagine how indignant you would have been? I probably wouldn't have agreed to seven years in the first place!

Laban had the audacity to bargain <u>another</u> seven years of labor with Jacob to win Rachel. Remarkably, Jacob agreed and fulfilled his promise. Now with two wives, Jacob needed a means of support: Laban to the rescue! For just six more years of labor, twenty years total if you're keeping score, Jacob could have a flock of his own for continuing to care for Laban's animals. Nineteen years is the longest I have ever worked in one place; I can't imagine patiently toiling twenty years under duress for a guy who kept changing my wages and terms of employment like Laban did. This story is almost humorous as the two men try to get the best of each other; after 20 years Jacob appears to come out on top. Read Genesis 29-31 if you want to see how all of this unfolds.

So how was Jacob able to stay patient and persevere? First of all, he knew exactly what he was working for. He "kept his eyes on the prize," as the Apostle Paul, a man accustomed to long-suffering perseverance, would later advise (See Philippians 3:13-14). Second, he accepted his current situation and did his best with it. Third, he used his smarts and planned for the future.

That's a pretty good road map for us, too. As the great coach, John Wooden, said, "Things turn out the best for those who make the best of how things turn out." I believe much of patience is acceptance of one's situation. Acceptance does not mean complacence, though. Acceptance doesn't mean we have to <u>like</u> our situation or stop working to improve it. While we accept how things are, we continue to visualize a better tomorrow, and we work hard to that end. This is exactly what Jacob did.

Joseph and Daniel are a couple of other great Biblical examples of people who patiently did what they had to do while trusting God. Like Jacob, they were true to their faith, which brought both persecution and blessings to them. In the end they prospered, though, because their God (that patient God I wrote about just a little bit ago) rewarded their steadfastness. God loves a patient person. I really believe that.

Sometimes God allows us to be tested to teach us patience. We can get into the weeds theologically trying to understand this. Just Google "the patience of Job" or read the book of *Job* (pronounced with a long "o" sound) in the Bible if you want to see a model of endurance. It will be tough to keep from feeling that God was playing a cosmic game of dice with Satan, with Job in the middle. Focus on the end of the story, though. Job suffered and even questioned God, but in the end he stayed faithful and God blessed his patience and perseverance. I believe He blesses us for the same things.

Being patient shows hope and trust. When we hope and trust in the Lord, good things <u>will</u> happen. I am not always the most patient person in the world, but I have learned to make the best of situations. I am thankful for what I have. I am alert to possibilities and work hard to do my best. I trust that God will bless me because He has already blessed me tremendously, and I try to live a life that will be pleasing to Him. It's amazing how a little gratitude and patience positively impact a person's life. If you are struggling in this area, I really encourage you to read about Jacob, Daniel, Joseph, and Job and about famous figures in American history.

May God bless you and give you patience!

Day 34:

Storms

I watched the rain fall steadily in the light of the streetlight and enjoyed the non-stop lightning show. I listened to the rainwater race through the gutters above me as I sat safe and dry in a rocker on the porch. I have always liked thunderstorms, the smell and sound of the rain, the rumbling thunder and flashing lightning. Wouldn't it be nice if we could just be spectators of the storms in our lives? We could enjoy the spectacle but leave it behind and go inside, where it's safe and warm, whenever we wished.

It's not usually that easy, though, is it? Instead we feel like we're right in the whirlwind, being buffeted about so that we can hardly get a breath. Maybe you've been caught outside in a storm before, the driving rain penetrating your clothing like icy fingers taking your breath away. Maybe you've had the dirt and grit attack you like you're being sandblasted just before the first big drops fall. Maybe you've seen the afternoon sky turn green then yellow like an aging bruise.

So, how do we go about building a shelter from the storm in our daily lives? What understandings do we have to possess to be able to find shelter in the storm? Let me offer a few for consideration: 1. Everyone has storms. 2. It's not the storm that's important; it's the response. 3. Storms have a purpose. 4. Even the worst storm will pass.

Everyone has storms

This is hardly a revolutionary idea, but it can be comforting to know you're not alone in the storm. I can think of multiple times when I was thankful to have taillights in front of me to follow as I drove through torrential rains or blinding snow. It was comforting to know someone else as crazy as me was out there. We all have drawn strength or hope from how someone else dealt with storms, or adversity, in his/her life. I hope that I could handle adversity as faithfully and gracefully as my mother did, for example. I hope that others might be encouraged by how I handle adversity sometime. If we see someone struggling, we can offer a word of encouragement, too. We may not be able to still the wind or calm the storm like Jesus did (See Mark 4:35-41), but we can help someone ride out the storm.

It's not the storm that's important; it's the response.

Sometimes the fiercest storm is overshadowed by the response to the storm. Iowa is relatively immune from earthquakes and hurricanes, but we get our floods and tornadoes. I'm old enough to remember the great floods of 1993 and 2008. Countless volunteers filled sandbags to try to help people save their homes and businesses. The great Iowa

National Guard played a leading role in safeguarding the people. Floodwaters eventually recede, but the compassion and kindness shown by others lasts forever.

I know the people of Parkersburg remember the outpouring of compassion after an F5 tornado ripped through town, leaving destruction in its wake May 25, 2008. Legendary Falcon Football Coach Ed Thomas helped rally the town, and the shared purpose of having the football field ready to go for the first game in the fall. My family traveled north with a church group to help assist with clean up. Parkersburg is just 12 miles south and 30 miles east of where my wife and I grew up, respectively. The town we knew so well was unrecognizable, even weeks after the storm. It looked like a war zone, with rubble everywhere. Visit Parkersburg today and you will notice the newer houses in that part of town, but you can't imagine the destruction unless you've seen it. In the end, though, the storm isn't the thing. The way the people of Parkersburg and thousands of others from near and far pulled together and rebuilt after the storm is the thing.

Storms have a purpose.

Even though storms can be devastating and destructive, they serve a purpose. We are in a rainy pattern right now in Iowa as I write this, and it's coming on the heels of two summers of drought conditions. The grass is green, and the water table is rising. God gives the Earth what it needs, and "the rain falls on the just and unjust alike" (Matthew 5:45). I understand we don't all get what we feel we need when we need it. I know that the rain that is a blessing to some becomes a flooded field or basement to others.

I would be hard pressed to articulate the purpose of a tornado. The meteorologists can explain <u>how</u> they occur (warm and cool air colliding, etc.), but the <u>why</u> of some things just eludes human explanation. God answered Job from a whirlwind (Job 38:1) and asks him, "Where were you when I laid the earth's foundation?" (Job 38:4, NIV). Storms have a way of reminding us that we aren't in control, as much as we want to think we are. Maybe that's one of the purposes of storms. I also really like Rick Warren's simple explanation I shared earlier: "God may send you a storm at age 30 so that you can handle a hurricane at age 60." Most of us do learn how to handle difficulties in life by persevering through them.

Even the worst storm will pass.

Storms can leave a lot of damage in their wake, but the worst storm will pass. In Iowa we might have to dig ourselves out from under a foot of snow after a blizzard, but we know the sun will shine again. Some people seem to endure one squall after another in their lives. Whether they are unfortunate or unwise, these people endure more than their share of storms. Even the most weather-weary person will enjoy peace and calm after the storms if he knows God, though. Even if his life ends in the midst of a storm, God promises an eternity of peace and light. Could there be a sweeter promise for someone battling through a lifetime of storms?

I began this entry writing about watching the storm while staying warm and dry. I believe, to some degree, we can do that with the storms in our lives. I am not suggesting that we should be detached from reality or that we can live some kind of charmed life. What I mean is that we need to realize that what happens to us doesn't have to define us. When we have a strong faith, we have built ourselves a shelter from the storm. What is most significant is what is inside of us, not what rages outside. The troubles in our lives do not need to define us. Hopefully our responses to those troubles do.

It's safe to say we will all face storms. The human condition is one of striving and suffering. It is also one of growing and loving. The more we are able to live life attuned to eternity and God's promise for us, the less we will be shaken by storms that come our way. Let's think ahead and anticipate those moments just a little:

My shelters in the storm:
1.
2.
3.

Provisions I can make for a rainy day:
1.
2.
3.

Have a great (hopefully storm-free) day!

Day 35:

Hit or Be Hit

Disclaimer: My seventh grade football season was cut short when I ran a finger through the belt sander in shop class, I didn't go out for football in eight grade because my best friend didn't, and I ran cross country in high school because my parents were paranoid about a possible football injury. I haven't been in a fight since fifth grade, and that one was mostly rolling around in the dirt. I am a squeamish person who hates blood, needles, and bugs; and I don't really know much about hitting.

But, it's a college football Saturday, I've watched about every Clint Eastwood, Charles Bronson, and John Wayne movie multiple times; and I was a pretty physical post player (How alliterative!) when I played basketball. I liked and sought contact. I initiated contact: hit or be hit.

I have always appreciated the bruising back that turned his shoulders upfield and delivered blows instead of skittering out of bounds. In the old days Earl Campbell, with his tree trunk thighs, ran over people. Walter Payton, Sweetness, could dish it out and take it. As a Hawk fan, I appreciate that Navy transfer and former walk-on Mark Weisman, who is so gritty and physical.

Besides liking to watch football and appreciating physicality, I just admire people who accept a challenge and go after it. I know there are times to be analytical and hang back; but once a decision is made, it's time to step up and go for it! Hit or be hit. It's tougher to hit a moving target. It hurts a lot less when you're expecting and initiating a collision than when you're standing there and getting blindsided. I'm seeing this play out on TV as I write this. The Iowa State Cyclone Football Team is trying to bounce back from a miserable week one loss to North Dakota State. The Cyclones are the aggressors in their game with 20th ranked Kansas State right now. They are pulling out all of the stops and just went ahead 28-13 on a trick play. I hope the Hawks are similarly aggressive against Ball State later today. This topic is awakening a sleeping giant in me, my competitive nature, which doesn't get indulged quite as much today as it once did.

What does it mean to *hit or be hit* for the average person in daily life today? It means being proactive, not reactive. It means having an action bias. It means stepping up and take responsibility. It means being willing to take a risk because you understand that's the only way we grow. It means taking a few lumps, dusting yourself off, and jumping back into the fray. This is the mindset that fosters resiliency and lets people really live instead of just existing. It's invigorating.

Once I have decided on a course of action, I like to be prepared and give my absolute best effort. I don't shy away from conflict because conflict is necessary and useful. As I have matured, I have come to realize that the old adage, "You can't win them all," is true and that failure is rarely fatal. When you're hitting and not necessarily playing it safe in life, you're going to get hit some, too.

I have written before about everything having its time, as Ecclesiastes 3 so beautifully communicates. I am not advocating acting rashly. If you want an interesting study of someone who vacillates between agonizing inaction and rash actions, look at Shakespeare's Hamlet. I advocate careful consideration and prayer, followed by decisive, committed action instead. That's how I have approached almost every big decision in my life, and, typically, the results have been very good.

I know people have different personalities and approach things different ways. People should be genuine and true to themselves. I certainly do not pretend to have any special insights, and I am not trying to be a self-help guru. I enjoy a challenge, though, and I think sometimes we surprise ourselves at what can be accomplished with a "go-getter" mentality. If you have something you've been thinking about doing but just haven't been able to pull the trigger, why can't today be the day you act? Why can't you take your shot right now? Do a little reflecting and get yourself ready to act.

Things I've been thinking about doing. . .

1.

2.

3.

Something I can do right now to be proactive. . .

1.

2.

3.

Day 36:
Bridges

Bridges are on my mind tonight, for two wildly different reasons. In church a few days ago I heard a sermon called "Building Bridges," part of a larger campaign by that name that the church is engaged in. Today I read in the paper that terrorists are considering—and have been for some time—attacks on major bridges. So what is it about a bridge that makes it a tremendous symbol of hope and faith as well as a target for terrorists? Maybe the nature of bridges and what they symbolize provide the answers to both parts of that question. Let's focus on two aspects of bridges, the implied promise of safety/stability and the assumption of connection/destination.

Most of us have probably walked and driven or ridden over bridges many times in our lives. Usually we do it without a thought or concern for safety. I have memories of crossing the "Swinging Bridge" in Iowa Falls on foot on many different occasions as a child. It swayed enough to provide a little fun and excitement, but I never thought it was going to come crashing down. I'm sure the commuters on the 35W bridge in Minneapolis seven years ago had no clue that the bridge would buckle and fall during rush hour either. The investigation determined it was a design flaw that sent victims to eleven hospitals following the disaster. In 2007, 140,000 vehicles crossed that bridge each day (www.minnesota.cbslocal.com). Thirteen people died and 145 were injured in the collapse (www.wikipedia.com).

Bridges are marvels of engineering and can be aesthetically striking, too. The Golden Gate Bridge in San Francisco took four years to build and opened in 1937 at a cost of $35 million. Since then its striking form has appeared in numerous movies. The Brooklyn Bridge is one of the oldest suspension bridges in the U.S., opening in 1883. It has been immortalized in the old joke, "If you believe that, I have a bridge I want to sell you." The United States is not the only country that loves its bridges and has them as lasting monuments. The unique Sydney Harbor Bridge, circa 1932, is called "The Coat Hanger" because of its arched construction. The stone Ponte Vecchio Bridge in Florence, Italy, is Europe's oldest of its type. There are actually shops within it—jewelers, art dealers, and souvenir sellers (www.travel.cnn.com) . Regardless of the style or age of a bridge; beams, arches, trusses, and suspensions provide the structure that make them last. No wonder terrorists hell-bent on destruction are interested in attacking these symbols of beauty and stability; the same things drew them to the Twin Towers of the World Trade Center.

Bridges wouldn't serve much purpose if they didn't take us from one place to another. There is an assumption of connection and destination. Without that, a bridge would be ludicrous. That's what Congress decided about what came to be known as the "Bridge to Nowhere" in Ketchikan, Alaska, backtracking on $223 million they had allocated to it. Actually, there was a purpose, just not one worth those tax dollars! Ronald D. Utt, Ph. D. called the bridge "a national embarrassment." The plan was to connect Ketchikan (population 8,900) with the Island of Gravina (population 50) and its airport. If I lived in that remote area, I suppose I would like that bridge, but the stated reason for it was to prevent people from having to wait 15-30 minutes for the ferry, which costs $6.00 (www.heritage.org). Most bridges have a much more obvious, necessary purpose.

Symbolically, bridges are a connection between the here and now and the future. Actions we take or relations we form now are often bridges to future opportunities. Sometimes bridges are a link to our past, too, and we are able to travel back over them for a nostalgic visit. Whatever direction we are traveling, it can't be denied that bridges are transitions, rooted in two different times and places. Sometimes we're over them in a barely noticed instant, and other times we have quite a journey.

That's the way it is with our faith lives, too. Sometimes people come to faith in a dramatic moment, with a "born again" experience. Other times people have a leisurely daily walk. I can't write about bridges without mentioning the most significant bridge of all time, Jesus Christ! Jesus is aptly described as bridging the gulf between God and humanity. It took Jesus, "God made flesh," to reconcile sinful, transitory humanity with our perfect, eternal God. We needed a Savior Who was faultless and worthy of worship; but it was the fact that He walked among us, was tempted and suffered as a human, that made Him readily accessible to us. He is the bridge that allows us to travel from a life on Earth, in which we live imperfectly and suffer and die, to eternal life in Heaven, where there is no sin, no suffering and pain, forever. What a beautiful, remarkable bridge that is!

Take a little while to reflect on significant bridges in your life, those you have crossed and those you anticipate. I'll get you started with examples from my life.

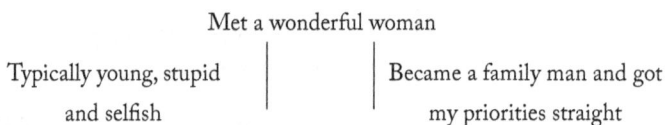

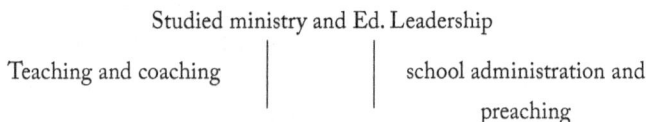

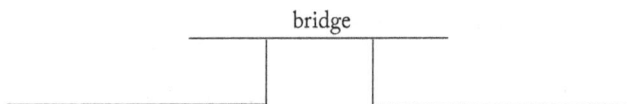

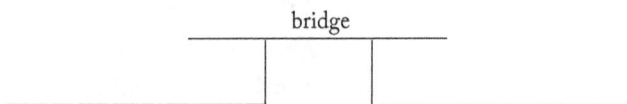

Met a wonderful woman

Typically young, stupid and selfish | Became a family man and got my priorities straight

Studied ministry and Ed. Leadership

Teaching and coaching | school administration and preaching

bridge

bridge

May God bless your journey!

Day 37:

Everything You Desire

How many times in your life, one way or another, have you had someone promise you, "You can have everything you desire"? Obviously the advertising industry does that continuously. So do the self-help books and TV shows. Even some of the televangelists, the "prosperity preachers," do so. Do we really think it is healthy or good to have everything we desire? I, for one, would be pretty much insufferable if things always went my way.

I'll use basketball as an example for me because it has brought me great joy and great heartache through the years. I was a pretty driven competitor when I was young. I took pride in people complimenting how hard I played and telling me I played with a chip on my shoulder. I desired a spot on the varsity team when I was a freshman. I didn't get it, and that didn't hurt my development as a player or my three-year varsity career one bit. My teammates and I wanted a state championship pretty badly. Two years in a row we lost in double overtime in the semifinals at the State Tournament and ended up third place twice. I still wish we could have played for a state championship, but I can't imagine how cocky I would have been if we had won it. In college I wanted to be an all-American and set school records. I almost felt I was owed that because I had passed up scholarship offers to play at a small college. Injury intervened, and more of my desires were left unfulfilled. I benefited way more by learning to deal with disappointment than I would have from more records!

Basketball continued to reward and disappoint me as a coach. I had a lot of great experiences, including coaching with my wife for eleven years. I helped build solid programs and had some wins and honors. I never accomplished what I thought I would in terms of wins, championships, and making the State Tournament, though. Coaching is filled with agonizing near misses and disappointments. Once again, I am fortunate that I never got everything I desired. That kept me humble. It helped me appreciate the relationships with players and other coaches. It helped me value competition, not just winning.

Whether we're talking about careers, material success, or our appearance, we don't typically get everything we desire. Hopefully we eventually learn it's not really about what we desire and us. As the Good Book says, "Many are the plans in a man's heart, but it is the Lord's purpose that prevails" (Proverbs 19:21, NIV). We have a God who wants to bless and prosper us. He won't deny us anything we ask if it is in accordance with His Will. As John 13:13-14 says, "And I will do whatever you ask in my name, so that the Father may be glorified in the Son. You may ask me for anything in my name, and I will do it" (NIV). If we believe that, then the task becomes aligning our desires with what God wants and intends for us. If we can do that, we won't be disappointed. We will be truly blessed.

Resist those voices that encourage you to chase any desire you have. God knows that is damaging to us, to grasp after material things and envy others. Why do you think we have the Tenth Commandment? "You shall not covet your neighbor's house. You shall not covet your neighbor's wife, or his male or female servant, his ox or donkey, or anything that belongs to your neighbor" (Exodus 20:17, NIV). We don't need everything we ever desire. That would not be good for us. How many lottery winners and former professional athletes do we see destitute and broken after their windfall? If we can learn to appreciate common things that bless us, like the freedom we have to worship, the relationships we have with family and friends, and the good health to work, then we are on our way to learning contentment and not seeking our every desire.

In the end maybe you can have everything you desire if what you desire is a close relationship with a loving God, meaningful relationships with other people, and the opportunity to serve and make a difference. You can see I keep coming back to my Big Rocks: faith, family, and work. I really don't desire a whole lot more although within these things lie a whole host of secondary blessings.

I wish you blessings and the discernment to know that you shouldn't seek everything your heart desires until Jesus rules your heart. I'm still working on that, and He's still working on me. God bless you!

Day 38:

Write!

I knew when I wrote, "Read!" On Day 31, I would be following up with "Write!" at some point. There is power in writing. As I quoted before, Edward Bulwer-Lytton introduced a lasting statement in 1839, when he wrote in a play, "The pen is mightier than the sword" (*Richelieu; Or the Conspiracy*). Earlier I wrote how important reading was to me; obviously I wouldn't be reading if someone hadn't written in the first place! Let me be clear, I am not suggesting that everyone has to be "a writer" in the commercial sense. Very few people can make a living that way. The great writers through history have usually had patrons, rich people who supported them. I am suggesting, however, that writing has benefits for everyone. Let's delve into a few:

<u>Writing makes it real</u>.

Why do you think we sign our lives away on a mountain of paperwork when we take out a mortgage or finance a car? Why do we have to sign waivers when we bungee jump or go up in a hot air balloon? "Sign your name on the dotted line," has become a catch phrase (long before Prince's racy song "Darling Nikki"). *Writing makes it real.* Handshake deals can be misremembered. Buyer's remorse could trump a verbal agreement. Convenient lapses of memory could creep in where written language doesn't spell it out. When it's there in black and white, it has some substance. This is why the common advice with goals is to <u>write them down</u>; then they become real. <u>Written</u> action plans are what take good intentions to the next level and allow progress to happen. Dave Ramsey, of Financial Peace University fame, insists on detailed written budgets. "Every dollar has a name," Dave says. In the interest of disclosure, my wife and I haven't been able to stick with a written budget, I don't write New Year's resolutions anymore, and I do not routinely write down goals (besides professional goals I share with the school board). I am a note-taker, though. I write to-do lists. I keep written records. I write about my aspirations. <u>Writing makes it real</u>.

<u>Writing says you care</u>.

I grew up reading hand-written letters from my dad, my grandma, and my aunt and uncle. My wife's grandma still writes letters as an octogenarian. I miss having my parents to write to, but I still send many hand-written cards and letters. Particularly in our world of quick, easy electronic communication, the physical act of writing says you care. You spend a little extra time, effort, and thought; and you communicate in a way uniquely personal to you, your handwriting. I have written this entire book longhand, in my unique writing, before I typed and edited it. I like my handwriting and learned to take pride in it by seeing my father's and grandmother's beautiful penmanship.

Within the last few days, I have had people come up to me and comment on my writing. A fellow administrator said, "I love that you write longhand." A teacher at the football game last night introduced herself and said, "It is awesome that you write everybody a personal birthday card. It seems like every day I hear someone say, 'Can you believe he did that?'" Does it take more time to write than to type? I'm a horrible typist, so probably not much longer for me! When you write a note or letter, it takes an effort that is becoming uncommon in today's world. Most people are busy and understand how precious time is; so when you take <u>time</u> to write to say thank you, express concern, congratulate someone, or just say hello, they appreciate it. I sincerely hope that when I leave this earth, I have left behind in my wake a huge volume of written communication that lets people know how much I cared.

<u>Writing is thinking</u>.

This simple statement, "Writing is thinking," is something I really tried to sell my students on when I was an English teacher. Writing with purpose to a specific audience takes some thought and skill. Writing coherently and engagingly requires being able to organize one's thoughts. This is true whether one is writing a single paragraph or a doctoral thesis. <u>Writing is thinking</u>.

I am not being elitist here. I am not saying that anyone who is not a polished writer can't think. I <u>am</u> saying that anyone who writes well has the ability to effectively organize his/her thoughts. You don't have to be a "natural" to do this, thanks to some genius who created the writing process! The writing process assumes that writing is going to be messy, like any other creative act. It also makes students slow down and think and gives teachers the joy of reading multiple drafts of student work. Make sure you don't assign something boring, teachers! I speak from experience. I am not advocating that you obsess over your grocery list or write fifteen drafts of your spouse's birthday card message before you get it just right. I certainly would suggest carefully proofreading and editing important communication like a cover letter or resume, though. If you are not confident in your own written language skills, ask someone else for help. There are all kinds of cursed souls like me wandering the earth, unable to turn off their internal editor. Ask them; they won't be able to say no.

Writing lasts.

In his "Sonnet 55" Shakespeare famously proclaimed, "Not marble, nor gilded monuments of princes, shall outlive this powerful rhyme." I've always felt if you're going to talk big, you'd better back it up; Old Will certainly did that. His plays and poetry live on centuries later (See Appendix K for a couple of sonnets that explicitly make this point that writing lasts).

Part of the definition of a classic is that it has stood the test of time. I find great power and wisdom in the classics, most notable the Bible, but also novels, essays, plays, etc. What is extremely interesting today is the reach and permanence of what gets written online. Shakespeare and Moses, for example, did not have an audience of billions at their fingertips! They didn't flip open their laptops to share a blog. No one could Google "The Pentateuch" or "Love's Labors Lost" and get a million hits in three-tenths of a second.

The World Wide Web's reach and immediacy makes teaching digital citizenship to children critical. As our recently exposed naked celebrities have illustrated, if it's in the Cloud, it really is public forever. In my mind this is a double-edged sword. We can all author our digital footprint or digital presence by what we say and do online. What does your Facebook account or browsing history say about you? Prospective employers are looking at your online presence, I assure you. Prospective love interests are looking. <u>Writing lasts</u>. People keep that cherished love note. They also remember that snarky Facebook post. Think twice before you write, but write!

I'm kind of a nerd; I know that. I think more about reading and writing than the average person. I encourage you today to think about what you could or should be writing. Do any of these fit the bill?

- Thank-you note
- Word of encouragement
- Love letter
- List of goals
- Birthday card
- Note of appreciation

Write on!

Day 39:

Grace

If I asked you to describe what grace looked like, you might describe graceful swans gliding across a pond, a red-tailed hawk doing lazy circles over a farm field, or a high jumper arching his way over a seemingly impossible height. I wouldn't dispute any of these as expressions of grace; I have enjoyed watching them all. I could add to these images, remembering the effortless bounding of a white tail deer over a barbed wire fence, the thick brush of a fox's tail swishing into the brush, or even an aged couple deep in love dancing together as the years melt away. I hope we all pause to enjoy those moments of true grace when we see them.

"Grace under pressure" became a famous descriptor for the Hemingway Code Hero. Ernest Hemingway created some very memorable characters that were calm and stoic in the face of danger and obstacles. Whatever challenges they faced, they showed grace under pressure. You may have known some people like that in real life, too. I hope we recognize those people when they cross our paths. In good times and bad, I admire people with grace. Regrettably, I am not always as gracious as I should be.

Let's shift the focus for a moment from grace as something we do to grace as something we receive. Grace is not good deeds; it's a gift. It's hard to explain how the gift of grace changes a person unless one has experienced it oneself. Max Lucado's book title *In the Grip of Grace* captures it pretty well. Once grace grabs ahold of you, everything changes. Grace leads to gratitude and eradicates entitlement.

My very simple definition of grace is "getting better than you deserve." A grace mindset is in direct opposition to an entitlement mindset that says, "I deserve that." I, for one, am very thankful that I don't get what I deserve!

I tell you, with no false humility, that I don't *deserve* the job I have; I certainly am not entitled to it. I do not *deserve* the wonderful, loving wife and two outstanding sons I have. I most definitely do not *deserve* the patience God has shown me and the sacrifice of His Son. Grace brings salvation. Thank God I don't get what I deserve.

The Bible says, "We love because He first loved us" (1 John 4:19, NIV). That kind of explains how grace operates. Someone who is truly in the grip of grace extends grace to others. Because we have gotten better than we deserve, we give others better than they deserve. No one deserves forgiveness. If it were deserved, there wouldn't be anything special about it. Forgiveness is not a natural human act. We want to strike back, not turn the other cheek. Proverbs, that book of wisdom, advises us, "Do not say, 'I'll pay you back for this wrong!' Wait for the Lord, and he will deliver you" (Proverbs 20:22, NIV). Even though we know judgment is the Lord's, we want justice. We want the transgressors to pay for their wrongdoings—right up until that very moment that we are the transgressors ourselves.

There is nothing in the Lord's Prayer that is there by accident. If you have prayed it, you have said, "Forgive us our sins (or trespasses or debts) as we forgive those who sin against us." How would you be doing on the grace scale if the needle moved in direct proportion to the grace you extend to others?

I'm working on it. I can be petty and judgmental, but I'm pretty forgiving, too. I can overlook a lot of shortcomings if a person's heart is in the right place. I know that I wouldn't want every misstep I've made to be held against me. When I mess up and sincerely apologize, I expect to be forgiven. If I didn't have forgiveness in my heart, I'm not sure I would expect it from others.

Of course, some acts are much more difficult to forgive than others. I know it would be difficult to forgive a drunk driver who killed someone you loved. It would be gut-wrenching to look at someone who murdered a family member, knowing that your faith said you should love your enemy. If it were up to us, we couldn't do it. Through the power of the Spirit, we can.

Jesus hung on that cross and said, "Father, forgive them, for they know not what they do" (Luke 23:34, KJV). He said to the adulteress, when there was no one without sin there to cast the first stone, "Then neither do I condemn you" (John 8:11, NIV). He said to the crippled man, "Take heart, son; your sins are forgiven" (Matthew 9:2, NIV) as He healed him. Jesus is why we can forgive. If you don't know Him, I pray you will reconsider and get to know Him! If you are feeling down, in need of grace and forgiveness yourself, go right to the ultimate source of forgiveness and grace, Jesus Christ. If you don't know how to go about that, start with this simple prayer:

Dear God,

You are the source of everything I have and everything I need. Right now I need your love and grace. Forgive me when I sin, and help me forgive others. Help me be patient and kind. Show me that the more I extend grace to others, the more I will feel your love and grace. Thank you for loving me so much,

Amen.

Day 40:

Don't Phone It In

Jerry Wainwright is my pen pal. Even though I have only spoken to him in person a couple of times through the years, I consider him a friend. When I met him, I was serving as his host for a speaking engagement at the Iowa Basketball Coaches' Association Fall Clinic. Coach Wainwright was the head coach at DePaul University at the time. I'm pretty sure it was 2007. Since then both he and I have had a few changes in our job status and home address, but we have stayed in touch, mailing each other quotes and articles we find instructive or interesting. I have a lot of respect for a guy who, as a Division I basketball coach, took time to do this (I'm sure I'm not the only one he corresponds with either).

Today I received from Jerry a little story about legendary St. Louis Cardinals broadcaster Jack Buck. Jerry wrote about Buck, "He <u>never</u> just 'mailed it in'." I usually say, "Phone it in," instead of, "Mail it in," so that's how we got to Day 40. Jack Buck is a Hall of Fame member for a reason; he always gave his best. It is said that whenever a game he was calling became a blowout, Buck would pull a $100 bill from his wallet and put it under his microphone. It reinforced that he was being paid to do a job, and he had to do it the best he could.

I love that illustration. Even if we have work to do that we consider a calling, that paycheck reminds us that we have a duty, too. It is a fundamental discipline to do our best when we don't necessarily feel like it.

Joakim Noah, a Chicago Bull whose effort and desire I absolutely love, took this idea of not phoning it in up a notch. A highly paid professional like Noah should be motivated to do good work out of professional pride. Noah's motivation runs a little deeper than that. He spoke passionately about playing for the people of Chicago. Even on a team that was decimated by injury and sporting a trade-depleted roster, Noah's effort and force of will galvanized Bulls fans and made the team a playoff contender. I was extremely pleased to see Noah named an NBA All-Star and Defensive Player of the Year. The Bulls' TV announcers love to proclaim, "Heart, hustle, and muscle!" when Noah makes a great play, and I'm right there celebrating with them. Noah doesn't phone it in.

I know the best compliment I ever received as a player was, "You work so hard!" It meant a lot to me to have an opposing coach make that comment after a game. When I was coaching, I tried to commend outstanding effort by opposing players as well as our own. I just deeply respect those who work hard, and I get impatient with people I perceive as lazy.

I'm sure there are a whole host of beliefs and assumptions behind my determination not to phone it in. Let me try to write my way into unearthing a few:

Phoning it in is disrespectful.

When we give less than our best effort, it is disrespectful on a number of levels. First of all, it devalues those we answer to. If I don't work very hard at my marriage, the message I send my wife is that she isn't really worthy of my love or best effort. I'd rather give up than work through any rough spots. If I do just enough to get by at work, I show profound disrespect for my employer. I show them that I don't care enough about the organization to give my best. Though I suspect lazy, unmotivated people don't realize it, phoning it in shows a real lack of self-respect, too. I have always believed we should autograph our work with excellence. I'm not sure who said it first, but I like this quote a lot: "Every job is a self-portrait of the person who did it. Autograph your work with excellence." If I'm going to put my name on it, I don't want to do it halfway. Most importantly, phoning it in shows a lack of respect for our Creator! God has uniquely gifted each of us. He expects us to develop and grow. If we don't strive to develop our gifts and if we are not good stewards of what He gives us, we are denying the majesty of His creation. People who fail to see humanity as the jewel of God's creation are much more likely to take a lackadaisical view of personal development. If there is no higher purpose or cause beyond oneself, what's the big deal about phoning it in?

Phoning it in cheats you out of great joy.

Theodore Roosevelt famously said, "It is not the critic who counts; not the man who points out how the strong man stumbles, or where the doer of deeds could have done them better. The credit belongs to the man who is actually in the arena, whose face is marred by dust and sweat and blood; who strives valiantly; who errs, who comes short again and again, because there is no effort without error and short-coming; but who does actually strive to do the deeds; who knows great enthusiasms, the great devotions; who spends himself in a worthy cause; who at the best knows in the end the triumph of high achievement, and who at the worst, if he fails, at least fails while daring greatly, so that his place shall never be with those cold and timid souls who neither know victory nor defeat" (http://www.theodore-roosevelt. com/trsorbonnespeech.html). Roosevelt knew there was joy at striving there in the arena. Carl Sandburg had the same kind of pride in Chicago, the "city of the big shoulders" and "stormy, husky brawler." I taught Sandburg's "Chicago" for years and had students write their own versions; I love the spirit of it (See Appendix L).

Everyone knows you don't win them all, but the competition, the striving, is invigorating. I never respected that person who, after a defeat or disappointment, offered the excuse, "I wasn't really trying anyway." I find that line of reasoning so annoying! Why would someone think it's better to claim apathy or laziness than to admit someone else was just a little better or smarter? I can handle not getting every-thing I aspire to, but I hope it's not because of lack of effort!

There is joy in work and toil. I know it's not always "fun" at the moment, but it is satisfying in the long run. I'm sure I'm not alone in noting that there seems to be way too much emphasis on fun today. Fun is transitory; joy is forever.

If you phone it in, you will never know how good you could be. Phoning it in places limitations on oneself. Unfortunately, many people experience limitations that are self-imposed, missing out o great joy in the process.

<u>Phoning it in sets a horrible example.</u>

Maybe you feel no responsibility to be a positive example. Charles Barkley, former NBA great, once famously proclaimed, "I am not a role model," years ago. I believe his ultimate point was that others, like parents, should be role models. Still, don't we all have an impact on everyone we come into contact with?

You tell me, would you rather be waited on by the slacker who is in no particular hurry to tear himself away from his smartphone or the friendly go-getter who greets you warmly the second you walk through the door? I love people who set a positive example even in doing routine tasks. I respect people who don't phone it in.

I hope you feel an obligation to the next generation, to your co-workers, to your neighborhood, to your loved ones, to fellow believers, to your gender, to your team, or to whatever groups you can think of. That obligation should be to set a good example. People draw strength and encouragement from others' good examples. They won't always tell you, but it's definitely gratifying when they do. Don't phone it in; the world deserves better!

Appendix A

1 To every thing there is a season, and a time to every purpose under the heaven:

2 A time to be born, and a time to die; a time to plant, and a time to pluck up that which is planted;

3 A time to kill, and a time to heal; a time to break down, and a time to build up;

4 A time to weep, and a time to laugh; a time to mourn, and a time to dance;

5 A time to cast away stones, and a time to gather stones together; a time to embrace, and a time to refrain from embracing;

6 A time to get, and a time to lose; a time to keep, and a time to cast away;

7 A time to rend, and a time to sew; a time to keep silence, and a time to speak;

8 A time to love, and a time to hate; a time of war, and a time of peace.

(Ecclesiastes 3:1-8 KJV)

Appendix B

#72 Death be not Proud by John Donne (spelling standardized to modern English)

Death be not proud, though some have called thee
Mighty and dreadful, for, thou art not so,
For, those, whom thou think thou dost overthrow,
Die not, poor death, nor yet canst thou kill me.

From rest and sleep, which but thy pictures be,
Much pleasure, then from thee, much more must flow,
And soonest our best men with thee doth go,
Rest of their bones, and souls' delivery.

Thou art slave to Fate, Chance, kings and desperate men,
And dost with poison, war, and sickness dwell,
And poppy or charms can make us sleep as well,
And better than thy stroke; why swellest thou then;

One short sleep past, we wake eternally,
And death shall be no more; death, thou shalt die.

Appendix C

THE SMALL TOWN DEPOT
by Craig Sathoff

The red frame building proud and staunch
beside the busy track
Was bustling with activity in time
a few years back.
Its agent was a shipping clerk, and stationmaster, too.
He was the chief telegrapher and
harbinger of news.
The depot was the very pulse
within the little town;
It welcomed loads of needed coal
and made the shipments known.
It served the people faithfully,
a guardian and a friend.
Their many needs to satisfy.
Their messages to send.

COUNTRY PRAYER
by Craig Sathoff

O hear my humble prayer
And bless, dear Lord, I pray,
The myriad threads in nature's cloak
That beautify my day.

I thank you for the lace-leafed birch,
The oak tree straight and tall;
The crimson- painted maple tree,
The golden gowns of fall.

I thank you for the time to plant,
The times of sun and rain,
The time to watch the fruits appear
And harvest-time again.

I thank you for the joy of friends
With whom to love and share,
For days of rest and holiday,
For days with toil to bear.

I thank you for the natural things;
For daisies in the lane,
And berries in the old fence row;
And gentle springtime rain.

O hear my simple country prayer
That from my heart overflows
To thank you for the precious gifts
A country person knows.

OLD FASHIONED KITCHEN
by Craig Sathoff

The kitchen is a cheery place
With trivets on the wall.
With an icebox made of solid oak
And a crank phone for a call.

Let's fire the old-time, cast-iron range
With corncobs from the shed
And fetch the covered rising pan
To start a batch of bread.

The cupboards hold a wealth of things,
From granite baking pans
To cherry stoners, butter molds
And churns to turn by hand.

An apple peeler has much use,
A sausage stuffer, too.
Assorted crockery mixing bowls
And tins come into view.

The kitchen smells of homemade bread
And fresh, hot apple pie.
As pleasing to the sense of taste
As to the nose and eyes.

It is a large and friendly room
And in its center there,
The hugest round oak table
Bids all to gather near.

THE GREENHOUSE
by Craig Sathoff

The greenhouse is a thrilling place
Each season of the year,
But I especially like it
When spring at last is here.

The little boxes row on row
Of seedlings to be set
Provide the surest sign of spring
That I have noticed yet.

Tomatoes, phlox, and cabbages
And pansies, deepest blue,
And pepper plants and broccoli
Are waiting for me too.

It's really rather hard to choose
The plant that I like best,
For each is lovely in its way
And different from the rest.

Petunias that I always plant
Along my garden way
Are there in every size and shape
And color bright and gay.

It always fills my heart with joy
And makes my spirits sing
To visit at the greenhouse shop
When spring is blossoming.

AMERICA BEGINS AT HOME.
by Craig Sathoff

America begins at home
With every child's need
For guidance and direction
In establishing a creed.

The roots that shape America
Are formed most surely where
A child spends the vital years
Within his parents' care.

Perhaps the close-knit family
Where each one has a task
Does more to aid America
Than anyone could ask.

Responsibilities at home
Build roots both firm and strong,
To guide our future leaders
In whatever comes along.

To work and strive is no disgrace,
Instead it is a joy
To build a great America
That cannot be destroyed.

This beautiful America,
So blessed with liberty,
Begins at home . . . its true success
Depends on you and me.

Appendix D

Lynda Randle "GOD ON THE MOUNTAIN"

Life is easy, when you're up on the mountain
And you've got peace of mind, like you've never known.
But things change, when you're down in the valley.
Don't lose faith, for you're never alone.

For the God on the mountain, is the God in the valley.
When things go wrong, He'll make them right.
And the God of the good times
is still God in the bad times.
The God of the day is still God in the night.

We talk of faith way up on the mountain.
Talk comes so easy when life's at its best.
Now down in the valleys, of trials and temptations
That's where your faith, is really put to the test.

For the God on the mountain is the God in the valley.
When things go wrong, He'll make them right.
And the God of the good times
is still God in the bad times.
The God of the day, is still God in the night.
The God of the day, is still God in the night.

Appendix E

The Heritage Singers
"I BELIEVE IN A HILL CALLED Mt. CALVARY"

On a hill far away,
Stood an old rugged cross,
The emblem of suffering and shame,
And I love that old cross,
Where the dearest and best,
For a world of lost sinners was slain.

I believe in a hill called Mt. Calvary,
I believe whatever the cost,
And when time has surrendered,
And Earth is no more,
I'll still cling to the old rugged cross.

I believe that the Christ who was slain on the cross,
Has the power to change lives today,
For He changed me completely,
A new life is mine,
That is why by the cross I will stay.

I believe in a hill called Mt. Calvary,
I believe whatever the cost,
And when time has surrendered,
And Earth is no more,
I'll still cling to the old rugged cross.

So I'll cherish the old rugged cross,
Till my trophies at last I lay down,
I will cling to the old rugged cross,
And exchange it some day for a crown.

Appendix F

THE DEATH OF COMMON SENSE
12-13-10

Obituary

Today we mourn the passing of a beloved old friend, Common Sense, who has been with us for many years. No one knows for sure how old he was, since his birth records were long ago lost in bureaucratic red tape.

He will be remembered as having cultivated such valuable lessons as:

- Knowing when to come in out of the rain;
- Why the early bird gets the worm;
- Life isn't always fair; and
- Maybe it was my fault..

Common Sense lived by simple, sound financial policies (don't spend more than you can earn) and reliable strategies (adults, not children, are in charge). His health began to deteriorate rapidly when well-intentioned but overbearing regulations were set in place. Reports of a 6-year-old boy charged with sexual harassment for kissing a classmate;

teens suspended from school for using mouthwash after lunch; and a teacher fired for reprimanding an unruly student, only worsened his condition.

Common Sense lost ground when parents attacked teachers for doing the job that they themselves had failed to do in disciplining their unruly children.

It declined even further when schools were required to get parental consent to administer sun lotion or an aspirin to a student; but could not inform parents when a student became pregnant and wanted to have an abortion.

Common Sense lost the will to live as the churches became businesses; and criminals received better treatment than their victims.

Common Sense took a beating when you couldn't defend yourself from a burglar in your own home and the burglar could sue you for assault.

Common Sense finally gave up the will to live, after a woman failed to realize that a steaming cup of coffee was hot. She spilled a little in her lap, and was promptly awarded a huge settlement.

Common Sense was preceded in death, by his parents, Truth and Trust, by his wife, Discretion, by his daughter, Responsibility, and by his son, Reason.

He is survived by his 4 stepbrothers:
I Know My Rights
I Want It Now
Someone Else Is To Blame
I'm A Victim
Not many attended his funeral because
so few realized he was gone..
If you still remember him, pass this on.

If not, join the majority and do nothing. (rense.com)

Appendix G

A MESSAGE FOR FATHER
by Craig Sathoff

I am no more the little boy
You bounced upon your knee
And thrilled with songs and olden chants
And tales of mystery.

But, Father, I am guided still,
Much more than words can tell,
By your desire to see tasks through
And do what is done well.

Your caring smile, your love of life,
Your kind and patient ways
Are guideposts which I shall attempt
To honor all my days.

The gifts you gave to your small son
Were not found in a store,
But, Father, now I use them still
Each year, just more and more.

Appendix H

ULYSSES
Alfred, Lord Tennyson

It little profits that an idle king,
By this still hearth, among these barren crags,
Match'd with an aged wife, I mete and dole
Unequal laws unto a savage race,
That hoard, and sleep, and feed, and know not me.
I cannot rest from travel: I will drink
Life to the lees: All times I have enjoy'd
Greatly, have suffer'd greatly, both with those
That loved me, and alone, on shore, and when
Thro' scudding drifts the rainy Hyades
Vext the dim sea: I am become a name;
For always roaming with a hungry heart
Much have I seen and known; cities of men
And manners, climates, councils, governments,
Myself not least, but honour'd of them all;
And drunk delight of battle with my peers,
Far on the ringing plains of windy Troy.
I am a part of all that I have met;

Yet all experience is an arch wherethro'
Gleams that untravell'd world whose margin fades
For ever and forever when I move.
How dull it is to pause, to make an end,
To rust unburnish'd, not to shine in use!
As tho' to breathe were life! Life piled on life
Were all too little, and of one to me
Little remains: but every hour is saved
From that eternal silence, something more,
A bringer of new things; and vile it were
For some three suns to store and hoard myself,
And this gray spirit yearning in desire
To follow knowledge like a sinking star,
Beyond the utmost bound of human thought.

This is my son, mine own Telemachus,
To whom I leave the sceptre and the isle,—
Well-loved of me, discerning to fulfil
This labour, by slow prudence to make mild
A rugged people, and thro' soft degrees
Subdue them to the useful and the good.
Most blameless is he, centred in the sphere
Of common duties, decent not to fail
In offices of tenderness, and pay
Meet adoration to my household gods,
When I am gone. He works his work, I mine.

There lies the port; the vessel puffs her sail:
There gloom the dark, broad seas. My mariners,
Souls that have toil'd, and wrought, and thought with me—
That ever with a frolic welcome took
The thunder and the sunshine, and opposed
Free hearts, free foreheads—you and I are old;
Old age hath yet his honour and his toil;

Death closes all: but something ere the end,
Some work of noble note, may yet be done,
Not unbecoming men that strove with Gods.
The lights begin to twinkle from the rocks:
The long day wanes: the slow moon climbs: the deep
Moans round with many voices. Come, my friends,
'T is not too late to seek a newer world.
Push off, and sitting well in order smite
The sounding furrows; for my purpose holds
To sail beyond the sunset, and the baths
Of all the western stars, until I die.
It may be that the gulfs will wash us down:
It may be we shall touch the Happy Isles,
And see the great Achilles, whom we knew.
Tho' much is taken, much abides; and tho'
We are not now that strength which in old days
Moved earth and heaven, that which we are, we are;
One equal temper of heroic hearts,
Made weak by time and fate, but strong in will
To strive, to seek, to find, and not to yield.

Appendix I

RICHARD CORY
Edwin Arlington Robinson

Whenever Richard Cory went down town,
We people on the pavement looked at him:
He was a gentleman from sole to crown,
Clean favored, and imperially slim.

And he was always quietly arrayed,
And he was always human when he talked;
But still he fluttered pulses when he said,
"Good-morning," and he glittered when he walked.

And he was rich—yes, richer than a king—
And admirably schooled in every grace:
In fine, we thought that he was everything
To make us wish that we were in his place.

So on we worked, and waited for the light,
And went without the meat, and cursed the bread;
And Richard Cory, one calm summer night,
Went home and put a bullet through his head.

Appendix J

KEEP YOUR FORK INSPIRATIONAL STORY
Attributed to: Roger William Thomas
(1996 *3rd Serving of Chicken Soup for the Soul*)

A woman was diagnosed with a terminal illness and given three months to live. She asked her Pastor to come to her home to discuss her final wishes. She told him which songs she wanted sung at her funeral, and what scriptures she wanted read, and which outfit she wanted to be buried in. Then she said, "One more thing… I want to be buried with a fork in my hand." The pastor was surprised.

The woman explained, "In all my years of attending church socials and potluck dinners, I always remember that when the dishes of the main course were being cleared, someone would inevitably say to everyone, 'Keep your fork.' It was my favorite time of the dinner, because I knew something better was coming, like velvety chocolate cake or deep dish apple pie – something wonderful. So, I want people to see me there in that casket with a fork in my hand and wonder, "What's with the fork?" Then, I want you to tell them, "Keep your fork, because the best is yet to come."

The pastor's eyes welled up with tears of joy as he bid the woman goodbye. He realized she had a better grasp of heaven than he did, and knew something better was coming. At the funeral, when people asked him why she was holding a fork, the pastor told them of the conversation he had with the woman before she died. He said he could not stop thinking about the fork, and knew they probably would not be able to stop thinking about it either. He was right.

"Keep Your Fork. The best is yet to come."

Appendix K

SONNET 18

Shall I compare thee to a summer's day?
Thou art more lovely and more temperate:
Rough winds do shake the darling buds of May,
And summer's lease hath all too short a date:
Sometime too hot the eye of heaven shines,
And often is his gold complexion dimm'd;
And every fair from fair sometime declines,
By chance, or nature's changing course, untrimm'd;
But thy eternal summer shall not fade
Nor lose possession of that fair thou ow'st;
Nor shall Death brag thou wander'st in his shade,
When in eternal lines to time thou grow'st;
So long as men can breathe or eyes can see,
So long lives this, and this gives life to thee.

SONNET 18

Not marble, nor the gilded monuments
Of princes, shall outlive this powerful rhyme;
But you shall shine more bright in these contents
Than unswept stone, besmear'd with sluttish time.
When wasteful war shall statues overturn,
And broils root out the work of masonry,
Nor Mars his sword nor war's quick fire shall burn
The living record of your memory.
'Gainst death and all-oblivious enmity
Shall you pace forth; your praise shall still find room
Even in the eyes of all posterity
That wear this world out to the ending doom.
So, till the judgment that yourself arise,
You live in this, and dwell in lovers' eyes.

(William Shakespeare)

Appendix L

CHICAGO
Carl Sandburg

Hog Butcher for the World,
  Tool Maker, Stacker of Wheat,
  Player with Railroads and the Nation's Freight Handler;
  Stormy, husky, brawling,
  City of the Big Shoulders:

They tell me you are wicked and I believe them, for I have
seen your painted women under the gas lamps luring the
farm boys.
And they tell me you are crooked and I answer: Yes, it is
true I have seen the gunman kill and go free to kill again.
And they tell me you are brutal and my reply is: On the
faces of women and children I have seen the marks of
wanton hunger.
And having answered so I turn once more to those who
sneer at this my city, and I give them back the sneer and
say to them:
Come and show me another city with lifted head singing

so proud to be alive and coarse and strong and cunning.
Flinging magnetic curses amid the toil of piling job on job,
here is a tall bold slugger set vivid against the little soft
cities;
Fierce as a dog with tongue lapping for action, cunning as
a savage pitted against the wilderness,
   Bareheaded,
   Shoveling,
   Wrecking,
   Planning,
   Building, breaking, rebuilding,
Under the smoke, dust all over his mouth, laughing with
white teeth,
Under the terrible burden of destiny laughing as a young
man laughs,
Laughing even as an ignorant fighter laughs who has never
lost a battle,
Bragging and laughing that under his wrist is the pulse,
and under his ribs the heart of the people,
          Laughing!
Laughing the stormy, husky, brawling laughter of Youth,
half-naked, sweating, proud to be Hog Butcher, Tool Mak-
er, Stacker of Wheat, Player with Railroads and Freight
Handler to the Nation.

Afterword

If you have found value in this book, I am thankful. I have been blessed to know so many great people who have helped me along the way and supported me. Being able to share my faith, my memories, and my opinions has been a blessing as well. I wish you all the best and would love to hear from you. My email is sathofar@gmail.com

About the Author

Art Sathoff lives in Indianola, Iowa, with his wife of twenty-five years, Cindy. Art serves as superintendent of schools for Indianola Community School District. Throughout his professional career he has been an English teacher, coach, bus driver, activities director, principal, superintendent, and pastor. Faith, family, and work are Mr. Sathoff's priorities and passions.

Art and Cindy enjoy attending younger son Trey's college basketball games as he plays for the Graceland University Yellowjackets. His college career began as older son Jordan's Wartburg College Knights basketball career wrapped up. The Sathoffs have been blessed with a wonderful family and great friends through the years.

www.ingramcontent.com/pod-product-compliance
Lightning Source LLC
Chambersburg PA
CBHW032053090426
42744CB00005B/199